SAFE SPACES

For Black Women

DEDICATION

First things first, this book would not have happened without the support of my husband of 22 years, Brotha Chad (as he is affectionally called)! He has been my rock, supported me every time I wanted to run away from unsafe spaces, and listened to every story without making me feel any other way than validated, encouraged, and elevated. Thank you to my three (yes three) daughters: Kayla, Klarisa, and Kara (The Ks)! My story would be incomplete without the three of you. To all my Sister Friends, thank you for your unwavering support! To the Alicia Nicole Presents: Safe Spaces for Black Women™ supporters, we are onward and upward; only great things from here! Dr. LaNysha, Sis, I messaged you and said, I want to write a book and you said, "LET'S DO IT" and we did it! Brittney Murray, my BRAND MANAGER, girl, you know how I feel about you, THANK YOU! To every Sis that shared their story with me for this book, I appreciate you. You made yourself vulnerable without question or concern. You trusted that I would protect you and keep you safe; thank you, Sis!

To every Sis that reads and feels this book, I want to say thank you. Please know that this book was written with love and adoration for Black women!

Love,

Alicia

Feathered Press

INDIE PUBLISHER

ISBN: 979-8-9851977-4-7

SAFE SPACES
For Black Women

by: Alicia Coulter, MPH, MSW

this book was published by:
Feathered Press Indie Publisher

TABLE OF CONTENTS

Black Does Crack!

Now Sis, let me put it straight: I love being Black, and there is no other skin I would rather be in.

But being Black still comes with difficulties.

Our entire lives we have been told that Black does not crack, that we as Black women can handle anything that comes our way. Well, I do not know about you, but my Black has cracked, and I've had to rejuvenate my Black with life's oils and berries more than once.

Recently, I started with a new esthetician who gathered my skin and made it submit to her hands. As I battled blemishes and lack of luster with my face, one of the things she told me is that when you work out or go outside, you must wear sunscreen to protect your skin. She also told me that the melanin in our skin is activated to protect it from the sun's harmful rays and heat in any form. So, while our Black is resilient, it is also delicate and worthy of protection.

Basically, our Black is activated to keep us from the drama the sun and heat brings to our skin.

When the esthetician told me this, I was shooketh and had to take a moment to process.

Sis, our Black does crack because when we are harmed by microaggressions, discrimination, physical and mental violence, we are in a state of fragility.

That state of fragility is what causes our Black to crack.

I'm grateful for my melanin, I mean, when I put on any color, that brown skin magic just sets it off like no OTHER.

Let's keep it one hundred. I love that dermatological research says the signs of aging are less noticeable on OUR skin compared to Karen's skin. This is dangerous because the Karens and their signs of aging or cracking help to provide space for white fragility and leave us as Black women in a space of being classified with less gentle language and classified as, "hard," "angry," and "aggressive." Forgetting that we are still women even though we wear signs of cracking differently.

As Black women, we have to assess individually how we present when our Black cracks as well as what methods we must use to restore our Blackness to its optimal status. For me, my Black cracks most when I'm working in a traditional workspace and having to manage workplace abuse, lack of promotion, and lack of support.

Workplace Abuse: My First Encounter

Sis, I will tell you, I did not realize that our Black does crack until I experienced workplace abuse and noticed how those encounters made me feel and my reaction to those encounters. My first experience with workplace abuse was the very first time I was fired from a job. The emotion that I carried from this encounter still resides in me even as I share this story with you.

2

I walked into *her* (you know who "her" is, sis… the YT lady's) office, looked to my left and saw the HR Director standing there. The YT lady was also known as the department manager.

"Oh, are you firing me?" I questioned.

"Alicia, please sit down," the YT lady demanded.

I took a deep breath, then sat down. The YT lady continued to talk but wasn't saying anything. Literally, she was trying to make me comfortable in what would be the most traumatic experience in my career at that moment.

As I sat there, I wondered, "What in the world am I about to experience? Do I want to show her my emotions and the level of frustration that I have with being called into the 'principal's office'? Or do I want to sit up like a 'strong Black woman' and act like nothing phases me no matter how much I'm frustrated on the inside?"

From the moment I entered her office, I can tell you, I really was nervous, but I kept my cool.

When she finally finished with the yick yak, I sat forward and asked her, "Am I going to get my referral bonuses worth over $5,000 that I am scheduled to receive in a few weeks?"

The HR Director came over and sat down in a chair next to me. She crossed her legs, put her hands on her knees, and looked me straight in the eye.

"Yes," she said.

And then it hit me: I had just won one of my biggest battles yet.

Sis, at that moment, I sat back in that chair, crossed my legs, and ignored everything else the YT lady had to say. By the time I checked back in, the YT lady told me that I could use her as a reference.

The HR Director gave the YT lady a stern look and shook her head.

"Alicia, you can use *me* as a reference moving forward."

Siiiiis, the way I cackled out loud was amazing to even myself.

After the meeting, I was escorted back to my work area to pack up my belongings. My desk was surrounded by all of the things I'd accumulated over a year—everything that helped create a home-like feeling while at work: my heater, letters and cards from loved ones, pictures of my family, artwork my kids drew for my desk, and cute little items that were given to me by coworkers.

I learned a very valuable lesson that day: only keep items at your desk that you can walk away from. When I had to carry those items out by myself, I wanted to turn to the HR Director as she was escorting me out of the building and ask her, "WTF are you doing? Why aren't you helping me?!" I did not do that. Instead, I reserved myself, but when I got into my car, I turned on Tupac's greatest diss track, "Hit 'em Up," and took my Strong Black Woman self HOME!

I Thought I Was Safe

I'm sure you're wondering how I got here, and if you're not, I'm going to tell you anyway.

4

It started with a YT woman (let's call her Karen) upset with me because I did not allow her to yell at me.

It's true what they say: startups have great perks. Fancy happy hours, catered lunches, fun events, French champagne free flowing all day, and decent pay. Every morning at the Los Angeles based human resources startup, Karen and I would have a chat that included our strategic approach for the day.

I must admit, at first, I had fun working with her! She encouraged me to work extra hours to make more money, gave me assignments that allowed me to network with great people, and helped me create awesome experiences for people who worked for the startup.

This utopia experience continued for about six months before it started to change. At this point, Karen often would work from home and leave me on-site to manage the day-to-day logistics of the contract we were managing.

One day, I spoke with a new client (a YT man). He asked me about a new contractor that would start working in his department. I told the YT man that I didn't know all the details, but I did know that we were negotiating the pay rate of the contractor.

Later on that same day, my phone rang. It was Karen, and she was upset with me. She yelled at me, telling me to never say what I said to the YT man again. I was confused because I had no clue what I said was wrong and when I asked, she told me, "You know what you did, Alicia!"

I was so upset, frustrated, pissed, insert any word that describes the emotions a woman has after being yelled at by her department manager.

I went back to my desk and told my work homegirl what

happened. We both tried to figure out what in the world was going on with Karen and what made her think her behavior was acceptable in the workplace. To think she could yell at me regarding something I said and not tell me what I said wrong was ridiculous!

For me, I was done with Karen and wanted our relationship to remain professional. I would no longer participate in company functions, strategy meetings would remain professional, questions about my family would receive answers like, "everything is great" or, "same ol' same ol'."

When she finally returned to the office, she called me in to apologize for yelling at me, but the damage was already done. Meanwhile, she has yet to tell me what I did wrong.

Weeks went by, and Karen kept reaching for the same level of communication we had before the 'yell,' but sis, I just could not give that to her.

What seemed like forever was about a month until the firing meeting.

The termination happened, and moments later I was in my SUV on the 405, jamming to Tupac, laughing on the phone with my friend. I couldn't believe I was literally fired, and I didn't even do anything. She took actions I deemed as workplace abuse, and yes, sis, being yelled at on the job is abusive and none of us should be okay with that.

Unfortunately, Karen could not handle the shift in our relationship and instead of allowing me the time I needed to heal, she opted to get rid of me. At this point in my career, I had no clue that Black women all over the country were being subjected to this type of behavior at work. Heck, I'm not even sure many Black women knew that Karens were yelling at us in the workplace.

Sis, It Is Not Us, It Is Them

After being fired, I went back to grad school to obtain my master's degree in social work. I took some time off, collected my unemployment, and focused on school. My thought was, *If I obtain a graduate-level degree, I will not have to deal with workplace violence.*

Well, I obtained two Master's Degrees, and the abuse that I and my peers experienced only grew exponentially.

I remember working for a large organization in the early 2000s, and my superior told me that she wanted to groom me for her job. Sis, I was so excited for the opportunity, for someone to think highly of me and want me to take over the department that I worked in.

Well, after telling me that, she then told one of my coworkers that I wanted to take her job! WHAT?! I never said that to her! She was the one who told ME she wanted ME to take over her role, but of course, everyone believed her and started treating me like a thirsty job-thief. As I type this, I laugh, because I wonder what I exuded to make them feel that I wanted *their* jobs.

I checked myself and said, "GIRL, this is not about you. This is about *them!*"
Sis, being smart, kind, and hardworking is not always respected as a positive attribute in Corporate America. I remember even saying to myself that I could play the character of the "Nice Black Girl" in hopes I could experience a more pleasant workspace. I made it my mission to bleach my personality so people would find

me easy to work with, an initiative-taker, someone who makes work fun for others, and more. Even in contorting myself to be this person, I still had to endure challenging spaces and places that did not accept me as a smart, kind, hardworking, and heavily educated Black woman. Corporate America continued to label me according to the common Black woman trope that they already clung to in their mind, continually asking me how many hairstyles I had up my sleeve; how I was able to afford the type of car I drive; how I was able to pay for the multiple vacations I took per year. I often had to ignore or laugh off the comments and text a friend experiencing the same behaviors as a way for me to vent my emotions and frustrations.

I can handle silliness and foolishness and even rejection, but why should I have to? Why should adults have the privilege of making others deal with their inappropriate, harmful behaviors? I often felt sad and depressed because these behaviors would make me wonder if the problem was me. I later learned it was their racism masked throughout Corporate America.

Are Black Women Really Safe?

Prior to the term "anti-Blackness" was a thing, let's call it what it is: racism and just all-around hate toward Black people. The reason why using the term anti-Blackness is important when describing racism is because it encompasses behaviors against upward mobility professionally and/or personally against Black people. Of course, the term anti-Blackness has allowed us to silo racism into a space where we can confirm where the hate and maltreatment are directed, toward Black folks.

Before I discuss data, let us deal with what makes these anti-Black environments unsafe for Black women. When we think about how we manage in the workplace and the world in general, we use our mind, body, and spirit to navigate spaces that are generally not made for us, nor are they made by us. When these spaces become toxic and challenging, our mind is not clear, and we struggle with executing simple tasks, reducing our ability to manage tasks both at work and at home.

Let us shift really quickly to our bodies; oh sis, our bodies! How does an unsafe workplace harm our bodies? Well, I do not know about you, but when I am stressed, I eat, and I eat, and I eat; whereas others of us undereat. Regardless of whatever direction you fall in, both are unhealthy and have long-lasting effects on our bodies.

Sis, our spirit is who we are and what we deliver to those that love us. When we are in a toxic workplace navigating anti-Blackness, our spirit is crushed, and we cannot give our loved ones what they need from us. In addition, we sometimes do not know what we need in order to manage day-to-day living.

One of the biggest crises that we have had to manage in our lifetime is the crisis of the COVID-19 pandemic and what the pandemic did to not only our physical health but also our mental health. To note, the data does confirm that during the COVID-19 pandemic, Black women developed mental health pods to help manage anti-Blackness experiences that were now in the forefront due to many of us being on lockdown.

One thing that I know is that we must not ignore what the COVID-19 pandemic did to us as Black women. As a public health executive, I cannot ignore what the COVID-19 pandemic did to us. Some Black women developed support systems to give mental health support in a for-us-by-us environment. For some of these Sistas, this was their first time going to therapy, and they were adamant in making sure that their mental health was protected during this once in a lifetime pandemic1.

Let me tell you, all my Black mental health provider friends were booked and busy during this time. Many of them stated the most common concern Black women was their dealing with the world's concentration on anti-Blackness and yet not doing anything about it systematically.

Although the pandemic is "over," Black women continue to deal with the aftermath of the realization that "Black is a Public Health Crisis."

Is the Juice Sweeter When the Berry is Black?

Before we go any further, let us address the thoughts that so many people have, *"BLACK DON'T CRACK."*

That narrative is false, and based on my experiences, Black does crack.

Our skin might not crack until we are of a certain age, but we as Black women do crack and have a hard time admitting it, or when it happens, no one within the workplace wants to accept and abolish it. When we do not admit it, and no one accepts it, guess what? Our cracks become filled with synthetic materials or behaviors that exhaust us.

What does that exhaustion look like for you, sis?

I know for me, exhaustion looks like bad skin, poor diet, no exercise, no personal relationships with friends—the list is endless. Just so you know, "Black Don't Crack" feeds into the trope of the "Strong Black Woman," and let me tell you, she does not exist in a space that is relaxing and peaceful. For the Black woman, stress is sometimes ongoing, and one stress after the other we learn how to put up with the stress, and that is not okay.

Black Women Do Not Feel Safe In the Workplace!

Here are a few stats that came from research by Catalyst in 2023:

- The darker the skin, the more likely the woman will experience anti-Blackness in the workplace. The data confirms the darkest hue is more than 65 percent more likely to experience anti-Blackness in the workplace.

- Nearly 1 in 2 Black women report that they experience racism more at work than anywhere else.

- Features that are considered stereotypical for Black people (you know the wide nose and kinky hair) can cause a Black woman to experience one of two things in the workplace: invisibility or hypervisibility. Basically, that means that your features will get you looked over for promotions and/ or notoriety. Your features may also cause YTs and those YT adjacent to notice everything you do: new braids, new nails, new car, new everything will not go unnoticed.

Sis, let's discuss what I mean when I say "safe."

Webster's Dictionary defines safe as:

Free from harm, injury, or risk; untouched or unthreatened by danger or injury; unharmed; unhurt; secure; whole; as, safe from disease; safe from storms; safe from foes.

This definition is all-encompassing. For me, the portion that is relevant to my definition of safe is, "**FREE FROM HARM.**" When I think about being free from harm, the thought is that this is a simple expectation, no harm in the workplace; you know, to be safe!

I believe that the only expectation we should have of each other is to be safe. I think we all have an obligation to ourselves and to those around us to be safe. I know that sounds like a simple demand from one person to another, but unfortunately, that is not the case.

Only you can voluntarily control the environments that you remain in. There is always the risk of not having the ability to control if you stay or leave, but when you do have control of your environments, please, make sure they are safe and free from harm.

Now that we have a working definition of what "safe" means to us, we can no longer ignore it: Black women lack safe spaces in the workplace.

While visiting with one of my daughter's teachers, we were talking about working in information technology (IT) and how Black women need to infiltrate that professional space more (he is a white presenting man). I informed him that I have worked in IT and with IT clients for years, and the workplace abuse that Black women endure abounds.

Did you know this man brushed over what I said and told me that if he can set them up to make over $120,000+ annually and they only have to endure a "little bit" of discomfort and 18 hours of peace, then it's ok?

Of course, my daughter was holding her breath because anyone that knows me knows this is something that I have strong convictions for (clearly, since I'm writing this book). What bothered me most about this encounter is that this is the belief for so many non-Black women in this space.

Black women continue to share their experiences in the workplace, and people continue to brush them off like they do not exist.

Sis, I want you to know that I hear you. I see you. I am you!

As I analyze the lack of safety in the workplace, I wonder if these settings are hazardous to our health. Could we equate the lack of emotional safety with the lack of physical safety in the workplace? I would say yes, we can equate the lack of emotional safety with the lack of physical safety.

How This Book Will Benefit You

Sis, my goal for you in reading this book is that you see the benefit in navigating safe spaces for Black women in your professional life. I hope the tough stories I share from Black women in various phases of their professional life encourage you to intentionally seek out spaces that only accommodate your need for safety.

I hope the experiences and tools that I share coupled with your judgment provide you the resources you need to eliminate spaces that are not safe and do not see your value as the queen that you are.

If your current professional space is not safe, you have experienced an unsafe professional space, or know a sis that is not in a safe space, keep reading this book! We are in a time where Black women need to confidently begin to create their own future!

Sis, let me know how you create your own future from the information you've received from this book; I want to hear from you!

Sis, you deserve validation, encouragement, and elevation as you navigate through professional spaces.

I wrote this book because these experiences of workplace abuse that Black women continue to endure deserve validation. Sis, if you've ever reported an experience of workplace abuse, I am sure you have experienced the ever so microaggression of, "They did not mean what they said," or "Are you sure you heard them correctly," or (this one is personally my favorite) you participate in an interview with Human Resources coupled with the interview of your coworkers to confirm if they have ever experienced you being abused, and then there is the final report confirming that after all of those steps, Human Resources has concluded that nothing has happened to you.

Sis, I see you, and I validate every component of this experience that you have encountered.

I want to encourage you by letting you know that you are right in your assessment of your experience; you have encountered workplace abuse, and you are being gaslit.

I know this is difficult to manage when you are being ignored and told that you are not experiencing what you are most definitely experiencing.

Let me tell you this, I've spoken to Sistas (some of their stories you will read in the various chapters in the book), and many of them say that their employer has ignored their concerns regarding their experiences.

I want to encourage you in knowing that your evaluation of your experiences is accurate and although I am not Beyoncé and will not tell you to "release your job," I will encourage you to determine your next steps professionally.

Determining your next steps professionally will determine your elevation holistically.

Sis, rarely do our professional experiences only affect our professional life. For instance, if you're a sis that works 18 hours per day, do you have enough time to workout, eat right, spend time with your friends and family, obtain 6-8 hours of sleep every night, and practice extensive amounts of self-care?

I doubt it, and if you do, you must create a program that assists Black women in obtaining the same life experiences as you.

For the rest of us, if you are working 18 hours every day or experiencing a less fruitful work experience, holistic elevation is necessary, IMMEDIATELY.

I am sure that you want to know how to elevate and I will tell you, one of the first steps you have to take to elevation is to recognize that there is a need to elevate and that is what we will do throughout this book.

I'll be honest, I've had to incorporate what I will refer to as VEE (Validation, Encouragement, and Elevation) to get me to the space where I can write this book for you.

The behaviors that I experienced while in Corporate America began when I entered the workforce in the mid 90's. Yes, I've been in the workforce that long, and let me tell you, stories that I will share in this book from my experiences and the experiences of other Black women will exhaust you. But, let me tell you, we are survivors, and we have the opportunity to encourage and validate you, and that is just what we are going to do in this book.

Sis, at some point I became fed up with the foolishness and decided that I could not do it anymore. Now, let me say this, *Safe Spaces for Black Women* is not a "quit your job" or "let me help you determine your next steps" book. This is a book to validate that your experiences are exactly what you thought they were. *Safe Spaces for Black Women* will encourage you on your quest of determining your next steps. *Safe Spaces for Black Women* will strengthen you as you determine what is best for you professionally.

My goal is to give you what was not given to me as I endured over 25 years of workplace abuse.

YES, ABUSE.

Let me make this clear, I am not a coach, nor do I move in life as a coach. I am a Black woman that encourages Black women, providing them with safe, luxury spaces without interruption from negativity, and that's what I want for you.

What do I mean?

As we continue to navigate through this book, I want to tell you, I am not here to tell you to quit your job, I am here to encourage you to know that you deserve more than an unsafe professional environment.

We as Black women endure so much trauma in the form of anti-Blackness, and we need to call it out and navigate it together with the goal of obtaining the tools that will support us in making SAFE SPACES FOR BLACK WOMEN!

Whew Sis, this intro has made me pour a glass of wine because it is heavy, and to imagine I'm just getting started.

"

Sis, our spirit is who we are and what we deliver to those that love us. When we are in a toxic workplace navigating anti-Blackness, our spirit is crushed, and we cannot give our loved ones what they need from us.

-Alicia Coulter

"

Sis, reflect on a time when you felt your
Black was cracking.

Chapter 1

Safe Spaces for Black Women: What is it?

Spoiler Alert: Sis, we are each other's safe space!

Not too long ago, I was brunching with a group of Sista friends (I promised I would not share any of their names), when one shared a current experience she'd had at work. Of course, the fancy cocktails were flowing and the food was good. You know, one of those good, good spots in the Los Angeles area. Sis told us all that she was ready to quit her job and move on from her dream company to a basic job just to pay her bills and find some peace and quiet to rest her mind. Of course, I'm fuming, because I am tired of hearing the hurt and pain that Sistas are enduring regarding their negative experiences within Corporate America. I am ready to down this lemon drop and ask for another just to help maintain my peace for a minute.

As I drank my lemon drop, and sat back with legs crossed, a Sista-girl look on my face, I thought, *How am I going to comfort her when she is done sharing this story?*

I tuned into the conversation again when Sis shared her experience with the male Vice President (VP) she reported to who head less credentials than she did. This dude told her that Black women do not study technology and that is why there are not any additional Black women in their department. At this point I'm pissed, because I belong to a Facebook group with over 13,000 Sistas at all levels of technology including the C-Suite.

Since 2018, over 160,000 Black women have obtained degrees and/or certificates in technology[2]. Knowing this, I was *kinda* shocked to hear that any professional would say such a foolish thing. Then, I remembered her telling us that this person was not the sharpest tool in the drawer. He was for sure an unworthy opportunity hire.

My Sis continued with her story. As she said these next words, not only did all of us at the table gasp, but the server also who overheard the statement apologized for gasping as she listened in on our conversation. My Sis told us this man said, *"Fox News is better than any other news station and they deliver the most truthful information regarding the 2020 President (sic) Election."*

Now Sis, gather yourself like we all had to.

I promise you; I took a large gulp of my lemon drop. If I am unable to speak, I can listen, and that is what my friend needed at that moment. I can say that everyone at the table paused and asked, "Are you okay?"

We could only imagine how she felt. Sis told us that she was not okay and detailed her physical reaction to his statement after he had uttered those ignorant words. She told us her body had felt numb, and sweat had poured from under her arms. She had felt feverish and clammy, and instantly developed a headache. She also told us that once she'd ended the call, she cried uncontrollably. At that moment, she had felt helpless.

We paused, as she paused. I promise you; I could see in her eyes the trauma that she had experienced during that encounter.

All five of us got up and hugged our Sis. We waited patiently as she took a moment in her safe space, with her girls, her Sister Circle. We did not interject any of our frustration, pain, or our own experiences. We sat and let our Sis present as the soft and sensitive Black woman we all desire to be when dealing with hurt and pain. I felt concern for my friend's mental and physical health, knowing that we were discussing this on Sunday, and she had to return to work on Monday.

Although I was aware of some of my Sis's experiences at work, I was not aware of all of them, and this was the first time I visually experienced the pain she was in. Seeing her face and feeling the pain through the words and tears and uncontrollable expression caused me great concern for her. I wondered how was she able to function day-to-day? She did tell me that she wanted to cuss everyone out, but I thought she was joking. After hearing her experiences and seeing her eyes, I knew Sis was not in a good head space; I was concerned that she reached her breaking point and no longer cared if outrage was the byproduct of her reaching her breaking point.

As we sat there, it was obvious that my Sis felt helpless.

How Unsafe Spaces Are Making Us Sick

Recently, I read an opinion piece in the Huffington Post titled: *The Workplace is Making Black Women Sick. Here's How to Make It Healthier.* I was intrigued by the title, and had to read what my Sis, Dr. Angelica Geter, had to lend to this very important conversation. Dr. Geter began the article with data confirming that in 2022, Black women were making $0.58 per dollar, which was $0.10 less than what they were making the previous year. That alone harms our mental and physical health. Dr. Geter discussed the root cause of our mental health in the workplace as being the stress associated with discrimination and workplace inequities.

In addition to being underpaid and the mental health stressors we experience, Black people encounter racism at work almost four times the rate of our white counterparts, and one-and-a-half times our Latino and Asian counterparts[3].

This racism mostly comes in the form of microaggressions, like the one my sis experienced with her VP, and being overlooked for positions after applying multiple times in various departments within the same organization. Other instances include racism in the form of statements like, "Angry Black woman," or "You're a little aggressive in your tone." Instead of addressing these behaviors, many organizations opt to ignore such instances and evade the "race talk."

Speaking of the "race talk," do you think Corporate America could handle the conversation confirming that many of their behaviors toward Black women originate from slavery[4]? For Black women, we have always been underpaid and undervalued when placed in professional positions in general. Even when we earned the "more desirable positions," we were still unsafe. This trend of harming Black women is not new, and the trope of the Black female slave continues to plague us even in the 21st century.

My mind is often jogged back to Viola Davis and her references of making less money than Myrle Streep and other notable white female actors, even though she is by far a better actor than all of them combined (in my opinion). Viola stated in her interview "I have more than a thirty year professional career... I got the Oscar, I got the Emmy, I got the two Tonys, I've done Broadway, I've done off-Broadway, I've done TV, I've done film. I've done all of it. I have a career that's probably comparable to Meryl Streep, Julianne Moore, Sigourney Weaver." Mrs. Davis continues on by saying

"We get probably a tenth of what a Caucasian woman gets and I'm number one on the call sheet; and then I have to go in and I have to hustle for my worth."

When I heard her speech, the first thing I thought was, "I have three degrees, over a decade of professional experience, and yet, I am still not enough. My Sisters have worked their way up the corporate ladder and they are still not enough."

We all have had white male and female counterparts that do not have a fraction of the experience and professional fortitude that we have and still, we are NOT enough. The feeling of not being enough is what I, my Sis, and so many Black women continue to feel in the corporate America space.

After my sis processed her pain through tears and other emotions and explicit words, the first question we asked was, "Did anyone else hear this man say these horrible things to you?"

You all know the answer… "NO!"

I then asked her, "Has he spoken to anyone else like this? "

Of course, the answer she gave was, "NO!"

At that moment, the table erupted with questions but they were short lived, because we knew that our Sis did not need that. Our Sis needed her Sister-circle to listen and provide a safe space for her to land. We did just that.

Knowing the demographics of her workplace, she is the only Black woman in her department. After we calmed down, Sis continued to speak. She told us she went to Human Resources (HR) and shared with the HR Representative that she wanted to file a complaint against the VP. The HR Representative scheduled a meeting and met with my sis, (of course, the HR Representative was a white woman from middle America) and within 24-hours had produced a concluding report stating nothing happened to Sis. She was not harassed. Oh, and the VP did not mean to hurt her feelings.

Black women going to HR to express negative experiences when interacting with leadership can prove challenging. One of the many reasons why going to HR becomes a challenge is that often our experiences are not understood and/or believed.

Sis was pissed and reached out to leadership in HR. She was in disbelief that HR would include the VP's sentiment to not hurt the feelings of our Sis in the investigative report. She escalated her concerns to the Director and received minimal support.

Now, after speaking to the Director of HR, she spoke with the VP of HR, who then arranged a meeting with the Director of Diversity, Equity, and Inclusion (DE&I). We all wondered why she wanted to meet with the DE&I Director, but we were there to listen only. During her meeting with the DE&I Director, who was a Black woman, she was gaslit regarding her viewpoints on diversity within the organization.

Sis, be patient with me as I share this experience with you. This experience was truly an, "every Sista ain't a Sista" experience.

When entering into this meeting, Sis confirmed she was excited and thought that her actions would allow her to advocate for all Black employees within the organization. Unfortunately, this was not her experience. The Director of DE&I had zero experience in DE&I. She actually obtained this position because she was one of the employees that was a member of the newly formed Black Infinity Group. From what Sis said, the Black women that were change makers thought the DE&I Director was a "yes woman," and that is why she obtained her job. Just think about that—the DE&I person was hired because she made leadership feel comfortable, because she would never hold them accountable.

During the conversation, Sis started sharing her concerns with the lack of TRUE diversity and how she shared those sentiments with the VP. The DE&I Director "informed" Sis that the organization was very diverse and that she was wrong. Just to note, Sis is like me and studied Critical Race Theory, but the DE&I Director had zero clue regarding her experience in that subject matter. Once the DE&I Director continued with her rant of pumping up the diversity of this organization, Sis gave her a quick lesson in DE&I. Sis did not go into great detail with us regarding what she said, but she did confirm that she told the DE&I Director that diversity does not equal white women and also confirmed that even if there are minorities in the department, when a single group of minorities is the majority of the workforce, you do NOT have diversity. By the time Sis finished telling us this, we were all laughing because we did not believe that the person that managed the DE&I space of this Fortune 500 Company did not understand that simple concept. Side note: Sis confirmed this woman no longer holds that position within the organization.

After this experience, Sis did not feel safe speaking to anyone in HR anymore, she knew HR was there to protect the company. Even though we know HR is there to protect the company, we often desire a safe space in the workplace where we want to feel protected. This is why Sis shifted to communicating with the VP of HR about the continued harassment from leadership within her department.

Sis said the VP of HR (a YT woman) made her feel safe and comfortable with sharing her negative and harmful experiences within the organization. The thing is, the VP of HR would meet with my Sis every other week to share her workplace experiences repeatedly where she would have to relive these traumatic experiences with the hope of being moved from the department. Spoiler alert! The move never happened.

Black Women in Corporate America Are A Superpower

Black women participate in the workforce at a rate of 60.3% versus their white, Latino, and Asian counterparts which is at 56%; we are the superpower in the workplace[5].

This statistic baffled me, especially since there are rarely any interventions that provide safe spaces for Black women. I was also surprised when I read that HR generally does not know what to do when discussing racism[6].

During the pandemic, when organizations were forced to deal with the biggest public health crisis, racism, they were encouraging employees to have "courageous conversations" with Black employees. My sis had to participate in these courageous conversations with the VP of HR and often wondered what would come from them. I can tell you, nothing came from these conversations but heartache and pain.

After months of having courageous conversations and negotiating with the VP of HR, Sis finally asked if she could transfer from her current position to another position within the organization. The VP of HR told her that she would help my sis, and you guessed it, she did not help her. She told my sis that she would submit her resume to a recruiter for asSistance. After submitting her resume, no additional asSistance was given and more harassment and retaliation took place from multiple employees. After all of this, my sis went on a leave of absence. She could not take the attacks and the fruitless discussions with HR anymore. My sis said she could not handle the toxic environment, and she was not alone. Most recent data is stating that over 40% of Black women who leave the workforce leave due to toxicity, not feeling safe, or burnout[7].

These statistics indicate that safe spaces for Black women need to be a major concern in Corporate America.

What Does a Safe Space for Black Women Look Like?

I know I keep saying the word *safe* and I want to make sure we dig deeper into that word and what safe spaces look like for Black women. In the introduction, I defined safe as *Free from Harm*. For a Black woman, a safe space includes an environment that is free from harm, one that validates, encourages, and elevates *Black Girl Magic*. My sis was in a safe space when she was within her Sister circle. That is a great space for our personal life. However, from a professional standpoint, do these spaces exist in masses within the workplace? Are there an overwhelming amount of spaces within the workplace that encourage Black women to develop relationships that are not inclusive of any other gender, sexual orientation, ethnicity, or any other identity except BLACK WOMAN? I know that these spaces exist in a minimal capacity, but is that enough? Do these spaces validate, encourage, and elevate us?

While writing this book, I did a quick internet search to make sure that the information I shared is factual; during my search, I easily found one organization at Emory University. I did find many Black Affinity/Business (or Employee) Relationship Groups, but they were not gender specific to Black women and those spaces are inclusive to those that are allies and supporters of Black people. Black women need spaces that are for us, by us,and supported financially by Corporate America. I have mentioned this before, but it deserves repeating. The murder of George Floyd forced so many people to pay attention to racism. Many companies made promises. However, those same companies did not keep their promises. Many Black women are barely surviving in the workplace. The lack of promises for not only DE&I but a safe workplace reduces our ability to thrive in these spaces.

After brunch ended and I was home, I could not stop thinking about my sis. I gave her a call to check on her. She told me she was doing fine, but was not looking forward to returning to work on Monday. I asked her if she minded talking about the "situation," or if she just wanted to have some girl talk. She proceeded to talk about her meeting with the DE&I Director. Knowing my experience, she told me the organization had developed Affinity Groups and hoped to discuss her participation in the Affinity Group with the DE&I Director. The Director stated that Sis needed to wait because the Affinity Groups were full. I paused because as someone who not only works in that space but also has professional credentials and experience in that space, I see that reasoning for non-entry as concerning.

Sis proceeds to tell me about this meeting and how the DE&I Director chastised her for reporting her experience to HR. After hearing this, I wanted to know how she responded, because I know how I would have! She confirmed she wanted to break down DE&I from an academic and practical stance to the DE&I Director, but she did not have it in her; she was tired and wanted to end the call. Prior to ending the call, the DE&I Director told her that she should make sure that when she reports her concerns to HR, her concerns are valid.

The DE&I Director then informed her that the organization is building a more robust program around their Affinity Groups and reporting to HR could harm the organization's progression towards DE&I.

Shouldn't these concerns increase HR's desire to provide a diverse, equitable, and inclusive space? I thought.

My sis told me she felt defeated and had zero desire to talk any further about this. She wanted to change the subject. After this conversation, my sis did not speak much about her job. She went on leave-of-absence because she could not take the retaliation and isolation from her peers. She felt exhausted and battled depression. Once she went on leave-of-absence, she no longer wanted to discuss the job and wanted to move on with her life. My sis is a smart woman with multiple degrees from respectable institutions, over 10 years' worth of experience in her field, and respected in her community. At this point in her career, she lacked validation, encouragement, and elevation.

"

For Black women, we have always been underpaid and undervalued when placed in professional positions in general. Even when we earned the "more desirable positions," we were still unsafe. This trend of harming Black women is not new and the trope of the Black female slave continues to plague us even in the 21st century.

-Alicia Coulter

"

Sis, do (have) you feel (felt) validated in the workplace? If so, what does (did) that look like? If not, how does (did) that make you feel?

Chapter 2

Validation: Why We Need It To
Achieve a Safe Space

Safe spaces for Black women in a professional setting is not easy to acquire, but that does not mean that we do not deserve them and should not seek after them.

One of the first steps to creating a safe space for Black women in the professional arena is to validate our professional experiences! Sis, before I continue, I want you to know that I see you! I validate you and your perception of every professional experience that you have had and are currently experiencing. While writing this book, one of the statements that remained on replay from Sistas that I interviewed was, "I wish my manager validated my expertise."

One Sista said when she received and completed the tasks from the executive she reported to, her executive asked her to contact her parallel in another department to confirm that she had completed her task correctly.

"Do you experience this often, Sis?"

"Yes!"

She went on to tell me how undervalued and frustrated she truly felt.

These feelings of not being professionally validated are not a phenomenon, and according to the data, Black women are given fewer opportunities by management to lead new projects and tasks. Additionally, the very opportunities that they are denied are those that equip Black women with the skills needed to navigate company politics for professional advancement within their current place of employment and beyond[8].

What Is Validation

What does all of this have to do with validation? Well, Sis, let me first define what validation means for the purpose of this book:

Validation: You are accurate in your perception of your professional experiences that are due to you being a Black woman.

Sis, let me be the first to validate you: The non-positive experiences that you are having in the workplace are due to systemic racism.

Oh, I dropped the race card! Yes, I sure did, and I did so with confidence! Unfortunately, society does not want Black women to receive validation, believing that our negative professional experiences are generally centered in the color of our skin, coupled with our gender. That's a hard pill to swallow, not because we do not believe it, but because we do not have control over the variables that got us here. Being Black, and a woman, is how we are born.

Sis, I do not know about you, but I would not change who I am for anything in the world. What I do know is that we are being punished for who we are in many places we work and/or provide professional services.

Sis, before I move on to how we can get beyond the need for validation, we have to manage the realization of what you're battling in your non-safe professional spaces. The question we must ask ourselves is, "How can we use validation to get beyond this space?"

First, we must recognize what we are experiencing. From the need to touch our hair, to the demonization of our characters as, "Angry or Aggressive Black Women," our experiences are legitimate, and we must validate them to proceed with encouragement and elevation.

The same Sis I spoke of previously shared more about her experience with her executive. Not only does she not trust her expertise, she then turns around and spills the *organizational tea.*

Let me break this down. If you are hired to complete certain tasks as a subject matter expert and your manager does not trust you, causes you to feel undervalued, and comes to you to gossip about the workplace, you are being abused, Sis.

The executive who uses the power and authority housed within their role and inadvertently holds you hostage, while sharing information that is none of your business and of zero value to you, professionally abuses both the power of the role and your vulnerability as their direct report. To confirm, we all love a little tea, and I can tell you, I've used professional tea in my favor more than once. However, when the spilling of the tea occurs between a manager to a direct report, this is where the abuse begins. Why is this abuse? Well, when a person (specifically a white, or white presenting person) has power and authority, their staff feels they must listen to them, generally having no confidence in telling them, "I do not want to hear this silly gossip. Please, stop." I've worked with clients to develop anti-gossiping presentations, policies, and procedures for all staff and leadership because these behaviors can cause damage and lead to harassment.

My good Sis from Chapter 1 experienced this perfect storm of not being validated in her role coupled with gossiping from her department manager on a regular baSis. During a 1:1 with her department manager, she asked to discuss the possibility of promotion or to take on additional tasks to elevate her current role and title. The department manager told her to ask the department executive. When my good Sis asked the department executive these questions, he told my good Sis to talk to the department manager. The merry-go-round of go to this person, no go to that person spanned over several months. When she shared her experience with Human Resources she was told, "Oh, I will check on that."

These stories that she has shared with me during the preparation for this book are jaw dropping.

Along with requesting a departmental promotion development, she asked Human Resources to support her with a transfer. She applied to multiple roles within the organization, and constantly received responses of, "No," or, "Let me get back to you." These instances continued while her white manager talked about her Black husband and Black children's hair being too difficult to comb. The manager also direct-messaged good Sis about her interactions with other leaders within the organization and how much she did not like the leadership of the organization.

What was my good Sis supposed to do with this information? Yes, she could have exposed her proof of leadership's behavior with her screenshot, notes, and saved information, but what does that do for the immediate abuse that she experienced prior to going on leave-of-absence?

She did not understand the need for validation or how the lack of it affected her professional growth until we spoke.

Why is Validation Important for My Life

When sharing my methodology for this book, I can tell you Sistas desired validation the most. Within a professional setting, validation of your negative experiences is priceless. Honestly, as we process through VEE, you'll see that validation is the only component that remains outside of your control. Your employer or other professional resources may not validate your experiences, but should you receive validation, snatch it up and run with it, so that you can start to feel safe from harm.

Sis, let me tell you, validation of your professional experiences is important for you to progress professionally and it may come in various capacities. While managing my negative professional experiences, I did not know that I needed validation, but once I received it, my professional caliber rose exponentially.

In May 2020, validation came to Black people by way of the Center for Disease Control (CDC) with the statement, "Racism is a Public Health Crisis!" The statements made by the CDC included but were not limited to, "racism is a system conSisting of structures, policies, (practices, and norms—that assigns value and determines opportunity based on the way people look or the color of their skin. This results in conditions that unfairly advantage some and disadvantage others throughout society) [9]."

I chose to directly quote their statement because this statement is valid for all Black women, especially the last sentence confirming the color of your skin will result in conditions or experiences that will disadvantage Black women throughout society. you read the statement and review the data that I have shared, it's easy to infer that the reference applies to Black women; Sis, this is true validation.

It's important to note that throughout my good Sis' experience, while on leave, she decided to file a case with the governing body of her state that manages workplace harassment and discrimination. Once she filed her case, she said, "I am validating that my workplace experiences are due to systemic racism that is inherent in Corporate America, and I am going to expose what has happened to me!"

She grew tired of dealing with all the drama at work. Although she did not know when she would return to work, when she decided to return, she wanted to ensure her job was protected. I mean, what organization would fire a Black woman who has filed a legal case against it? Well, she learned quickly that her organization did not care that she had filed a case. Within a month after filing, while on disability, she was fired. She was never clear about the organization's reasons for firing her, but from what she told me, they fired her because they wanted her to return to work. When she told the Sistas this at our monthly brunch, we found it difficult to believe! I can tell you, I ordered Lemon Drops again! As the story regarding this employer continued to grow, I remained in disbelief. Nearly seven months passed before my good Sis gave us any additional information regarding her previous employer. When she brought up the subject, it was truly a dump.

When my good Sis arrived at brunch after seven months without news after having been fired, she had a big smile on her face. We noticed her excitement and wondered what in the world had happened, yet, we were happy to see her smile. She sat down and ordered two bottles of the finest champagne on the menu, said that brunch was her treat, and that we could order whatever we wanted. We looked at each other bewildered. Where had the money come from for this fine dining experience, and where in the world did the joy we saw on our good Sis's face come from? I mean, we order like drug dealers when we go out, so this was not a new experience. However, we split the bill evenly and go on about our business. Was it a new man, a new car, or something else that gave her joy?

Once the champagne was delivered and poured, my good Sis told us that the company that fired her settled her case for six figures and she did not have to pay anything to an attorney! My jaw hit the floor! My good Sis received her validation by way of her state of residence, and I could not be more excited for her. She told us the organization had to make changes to their policies and procedures AND facilitate multiple training sessions for organizational leaders regarding best practices.

The state also reserved the right to review within 365 days of the executed contract. The organization followed through with regard to the multiple training sessions.

Sis, we hollered, screamed, cried and jumped up and down for our Sis like we were in a Baptist church on Resurrection Sunday! We did not care if everyone was looking at us. We knew our good Sis deserved the blessing of validation. And, because she received it, we all received it!

This was the best brunch our Sister circle had in a long time. Many of us had suffered professionally. The fact that our good Sis had received validation made her validation beautiful for all of us. Lemon drops and bubbles continued to freely flow!!

Do the Marginalized and Vulnerable Receive Validation?

As I prepared to write this book, I met with a select group of Sistas from different industries and agreed to keep their names and other personally identifying information confidential. I would never place these Sistas in harm's way. My most validating conversations came from women who worked in healthcare.

The healthcare system is not the best for Black women, especially when it comes to Black women surviving childbirth. A 2014–2016 national study on pregnancy-related deaths in the US concluded that Black women have an average maternal mortality rate of 41.7 women per 100,000 pregnancies[10], compared to White women who average 13.4, making the maternal death rate for Black women 243% higher than for White women.

Knowing this now, I kinda feel foolish for thinking that my workplace environment would provide me any type of safety or validation. A Sis that I spoke with who worked for a national healthcare organization remained loyal to her job until finally, she had a breaking point. She quit, six figures down the drain! . What caused the breaking point, you ask? Let me tell you, it was the straw breaking the camel's back exemplified. Sis was tired of her director's lack of support—a director who took leaves-of-absence every three to four months leaving her work behind for Sis to complete without a salary increase. Well wait, Sis said her bonus was $500!

Sis worked for a national healthcare brand that is considerably worth over $15,000,000,000; the company's net worth has increased tenfold since 2020. Sis has been going to a therapist for years now. Her therapist and I have encouraged a leave-of-absence for some time. When I heard that she was taking it, I asked her how she came to the decision. Sis told me she recognized she had given many years of service to an organization that did not care about her health and wellbeing. She confirmed her leave-of-absence would last for a few months. After her leave, she planned to resign and obtain employment from an organization that paid considerably less and take on an additional job to maintain her mortgage payment. I was shocked but held zero judgment. I, too, have made the decision to gamble with my livelihood by reducing my salary in order to obtain and maintain peace.

Once Sis went on leave-of-absence, she learned that less than two days later, two employees within her department were brought in to manage her workload. I'm guessing that is not the first time that you've heard of this happening; a Black woman exiting a role and two or three other people being brought in to fill her role.

Does Validation Always Help

Sometimes, people want to provide validation for your experiences because it makes them feel better. Their desire to validate your experiences are not rooted in your needs but rooted in their desire for their version of allyship. Over 80% of white women believe they provide adequate "allyship" to Black women within the workplace while only 10% of Black women feel they are receiving adequate support and allyship from white women in the workplace[11].

Clearly there is a disconnect between white women believing that they show up as supportive allies to Black women, and Black women confirming that they are not receiving the support they need. I spoke with another Sis, employed by a predominantly white organization that is respected as an incubator of research and design within all areas and fields. The space this Sis works as a PhD level researcher over a very influential project.

Recently, the organization hired a consultant to shine a light on the weaknesses and strengths associated with the research team and to confirm next steps to keep the research on track. When PhD Sis and I get on the phone, we *kee-kee* and *ha-ha* about our experiences within the workplace like none other. Before we started this convo, PhD Sis said, "I need to take a copule of Motrin before we start this conversation."

First, I had no clue PhD Sis was under this much stress, and I was concerned that this job was too much for her at that moment..

Then she dropped this bomb on me as I sat in my office, away from my house and the chatter of my husband and two of my three daughters.

PhD Sis is a mid level expert on the research team and she reports to an executive that is, of course, a white woman. PhD Sis confirmed when she spoke with the consultant, she gave her an earful of information regarding the Program Director and how she absolutely hates reporting into her. The day before the entire department met with the consultant, I spoke with PhD Sis and she was excited to hear the outcome of the consultant's assessment. She went to the office for the meeting instead of attending the meeting virtually.

Now, back to the gummy infused conversation. PhD Sis dropped the biggest bomb on me! She confirmed that the consultant said that the organization needs to hire someone that is organizationally between her and the Program Director. Let that sink in for a moment. PhD Sis confirmed that her relationship with the Program Director was not the best. Sis had shared multiple issues that she encountered when reporting to the Program Director. The consultant's recommendation had been to add another layer of supervision to the organizational structure.

Immediately, I asked PhD Sis to stop and to repeat herself. I wanted to ensure that I had heard her correctly. She repeated herself and I remained in disbelief. Her situation illustrated validation gone wrong and the fact that validation must include the requests of the Sista needing validation. The consultant clearly had heard what PhD Sis said and had understood her experience. With that said, the consultant missed the bar, failing to supply the validation required for upward mobility. Instead, her recommendation pushed Sis farther down in the organizational hierarchy. That type of move did not constitute validation.

I asked Sis how she felt.

"It doesn't matter where we sit within the organization. We will see systematic oppression and racism, and that is what I am experiencing now."

I had to sit on that for a minute and try my hardest not to turn this conversation into a therapy session, because she is my friend and a woman of great academic pedigree. During the call, she reminded me that she had been trained by top tier academicians in public health across the world. Even with her credentials, experience, and industry respect, she was not being considered for promotion. She holds respect across the nation for her research, yet the lack of respect and borderline bullying from her academic institution and her program, where she currently works, remains rooted in racism, gender bias, and systematic oppression.

As our conversation continued, PhD Sis confirmed that she called her sibling, a well connected person. She told him, "I need a new job!"

PhD Sis is driven by her research and the program is as successful as it is because of her passion and professional connections. She knew that her leaving the program could harm the research, which underscores how far she had been pushed to come to the conclusion that as we said on the call, "that is not our problem."

When I hung up with my PhD Sis, who developed a plan to leave her research for peace of mind, I immediately thought of my other Sis who took a leave-of-absence and a position that paid less for peace of mind.

I wondered why do Black women have to dim their lights and uproot professionally in order to find peace-of-mind? After pondering that for a while, I was reminded of the words of one of my Sistas."They will burn down an entire city to protect a white woman, and I will allow the entire project to fail to protect this Black woman."

When you are able to exit a space that is not safe for you without worry or care, you validate your worth, and need not to continue giving environments the best of you.

Sis, validation may not come in the way you desire it, but it will come, and when it does, it's like a lightbulb turns on. Truthfully, how it comes matters less than the fact that validation is here and ready for you to move on to your next professional endeavor. Be encouraged, the Sistas I spoke to in this chapter who have received validation, sustain a level of peace, knowing that their perception of their experiences proved correct. Their perception provided them the confidence to make decisions regarding next steps within their careers.

How Can Validation Encourage Money Moves

Validation in the form of financial payout did a wonderful thing for my good Sis with the racist executive who thought Fox News was the be-all and end-all of news coverage. Her experience also did a good thing for our entire Sister circle. To have the opportunity to experience a Black woman win against a corporate giant yields a feeling of success for the entire Black Woman Delegation! We have talked about this win for years and truly are of the "a win is a win" philosophy. Wins never get old and when you win once, in your mind, you can win again.

Once you receive validation, you might obtain the ability to move more fluidly in your workplace. You might gain the confidence you need to develop a strategy that will asSist you in building a new business, applying for a new job, or taking some time off to regroup and clear your mind. Regardless of what others say about your perception of your professional experiences, all that matters is your perception and your ability to use the validation that you receive to encourage you to be of the *can't stop, won't stop* philosophy both professionally and financially.

I know you want to know what my good Sis did with that money! Well, when we had our brunch, before I started writing, she told us that she decided to invest in real estate and take some time off to determine her next business venture. I asked her if she planned to return to Corporate America. She said, "Probably not." The last job mentally drained her, and she no longer felt able to handle the blatant racism she experienced at the hands of previous employers.

Sis, receiving validation that your professional experiences are due to systemic racism is not easy and can cause you to look at your employer with an ever more intense side-eye. Although the opportunity existed for my good Sis to return to her job after she received validation for her experience, she opted not to. She decided to create a new environment for herself professionally rather than returning to Corporate America and an abusive workplace.

Sis, remember, I am not telling anyone to *release their job*. My goal is to share experiences from other women that have obtained their VEE and are now thriving mentally, physically, and financially.

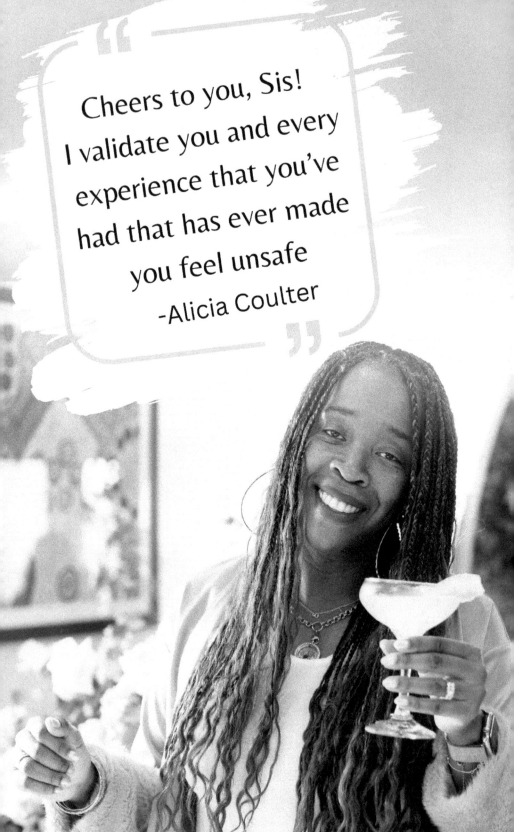

Sis, when you are not safe, what does encouragement look like for you?

Chapter 3

Encouragement

Sis, let me encourage you: You are Black Girl Magic personified. You got this! You are everything they wish they could be and everything they are not.

Encouragement was the hardest part of VEE for me. I did not think that I would ever feel encouraged as a professional woman.

This book is not a memoir. BUT I opened with my first experience of workplace abuse. I want to confirm that I did not obtain Validation, Encouragement, and Elevation (VEE) quickly. My path to VEE was not short. I did not bypass one step on my mission to escape workplace abuse. Mine has been a mission of great proportion, and I am proud of my journey.

Professional success is important to me, and I find it weird and disturbing when others prefer, I not succeed because of the color of my skin. Knowing that there are people out there who feel this way is what inspired me to create Safe Spaces for Black Women™.

What is Encouragement

Encouragement: Encouragement happens when you feel

supported! In addition to feeling supported, you must acknowledge that support may not always come from outside forces. Sometimes, you must encourage yourself as you navigate challenging experiences throughout your professional career. Professionally, I had support and encouragement from my husband and friends, but there are certain aspects of my career navigation where the responsibility of support rested solely with me.

To set the stage, my mission to VEE began in 2016, seven years ago.

During the introduction, I told a story about my first experience being terminated. One thing I did not share was that the experience did not put me on the path to VEE. I did not possess the tools to manage the various professional experiences leading up to my pathway transformation. I did not realize that VEE was the tool that I used until I decided to validate Black women's negative experiences in Corporate America.

I Had to Encourage Myself

In 2016, I reached the point in my career where I thought I was on my path toward executive leadership. I did the right things. I obtained my master's in social work. I then started my career path in healthcare as a Clinical Social Worker with the goal of gaining enough healthcare experience to propel me into Corporate America, a space that was centered in program management. Well, let's just say, it was not as easy as I thought it would be.

Sidenote: As I continue to share, you will notice that some of these stories sound the same. Unfortunately, Black women's stories of workplace abuse are sometimes paralleled.

During that time, I shared an office with other clinical professionals in the Case Management Department. We were (I thought) a tight unit. We would laugh about the silliness that occurred at work, and we worked together to keep our patients safe from systemic racism and healthcare fraud. I thought I had found my place and my people.

One day, while in the office with my colleagues, we all complained in unison about leadership making what we thought were illegal changes to policies and procedures. Until this point, we were supported by our department director. I felt protected from any type of professional harm within this environment. By all appearances, I believed I worked in a safe space for a Black woman. The director, a white woman, seemed a true ally for Black women and desired to elevate me professionally; I thought I had arrived.

What made her an ally? She told me that she wanted to support me in any way that I needed and would work to elevate me professionally by giving me projects to manage within the hospital. She also would intentionally stand near my office as a buffer if others challenged my decision making regarding a patient. At that point in my career, that was all that I needed!

A week or so after the complaining session, my colleagues and I were called into the conference room by the CEO, a loud and proud Republican who loved Ronald Reagan unapologetically. Remember, this is 2016, and President Obama was in office, so you know he was mad about all things anti-BLACK!

When You Realize Your Blackness is Unsafe

Upon being called into the conference room, the CEO informed us that our department director was no longer with the organization (we later found out that she was fired for supporting our team) and we would report to this woman who was a thorn in my side, the Chief Nursing Officer (CNO). She was a short woman who talked fast, functioned outside of her capacity, and possessed zero understanding of my role as a Clinical Social Worker within a hospital setting. I knew at that moment my career within that space was doomed.

While the Republican CEO had continued to speak, my thought had been, "I am going to challenge him regarding the policies and procedures my colleagues and I had complained about collectively." At the time, I had believed, "these women will have my back and chime in to support me when appropriate."

JOKE'S ON ME!

When the Republican CEO had finished his white man rant, I spoke up, thinking I would receive the backing of the rest of my colleagues. You know, I had played the part of the Black woman who opted to speak-out for everyone, with the thought that at least one person would have had my back.

Sis, this was the first time I had done so, and it for sure was the last. Of course, when I spoke up, not one of my complaining colleagues showed support. They left me hanging. This was impactful and hurtful, because I had trusted these women. We had gone to lunch together, exchanged Christmas gifts, and spent time together, sharing our professional and personal goals. Additionally, when one of the ladies had become ill at work, I had driven her to a neighboring, more efficient hospital even though doing so had been against company policy.

After I spoke-up regarding the policy and procedure, the Republican-loving CEO asked if anyone else agreed with what I had said. Not only did no one agree, one of the ladies had stated, "I'm happy with the direction this is going."

I felt shaken, and numb. My body felt hot, my head hurt and I wanted to scream!

When we returned to the office, I remained quiet and stayed to myself for days on end. The ladies tried to engage me in conversation. I barely responded. I sat in the office with my headphones on and listened to gospel music to ensure I remained in a positive space. Although I wore headphones, I kept my music low enough to hear them call my name. I acted as though I could not hear them, because I did not want to engage in conversation with these women.

A few weeks after this situation occurred, I received a verbal warning from the Republican CEO, regarding a rumor that had spread through the hospital, regarding me reporting a violation.

Let me tell you what the violation was; a physician informed an adult patient's mother that he was HIV positive. HIV positive patients are of a special protected class, therefore, disclosing their diagnosis without their permission comes with great penalty both to the person who shared the diagnosis and the facility. Now, if I did not manage the violation within the laws of Los Angeles County, the State of California, and the federal government, I would have placed my credentials and those of all parties involved at risk.

I did not report the violation. Instead, I called the governing agency to receive consultation regarding the incident.

For those of you who do not work in healthcare at the clinical level, when there is an incident that violates the law or policy set by the government or the hospital, the Clinical Social

Worker is informed and should assess the next steps. In certain circumstances, the Clinical Social Worker must consult with a colleague or a governing body outside the purview of the hospital. That is exactly what I did. Well, someone reported my actions to the Republican CEO. Within 24 hours, I had been called to his office for a meeting.

I waited outside the office, where I found the Human Resources Coordinator. I asked, "Are you here to facilitate my termination or a write-up?"

She did not answer me, but her eyes communicated a look of oh, no. The CEO's assistant called us into his office where we took our seats. I looked at his desk, reminded of my interview and how uncomfortable I had felt gazing at the prominently placed picture of Ronald Regan. I reconciled myself to an IDGAF attitude, yet, then realized I had to snap out of it because he was talking to me.

The details of my verbal warning included multiple issues. The one that stood out had been his allegation that I had been "mean" to the CNO. He said, "That will not be tolerated." I remember shutting out his voice (please note this has been rephrased to avoid the split infinitive "tuning him out."), and then saying to myself, "Girl, get out of this job now." I found it hilarious that he had cited personal emotions without examples. While tuning him out, I finished the pep talk with myself.

The only thing on my mind had been to tell that CEO that I had no intention of ever signing the document he had placed before me. Instead, my thought had been to get out of his office, go to my car, and call my husband. Once he had completed his monologue, I advocated for myself. I told him that he had no clue what he was talking about and that I would not sign the document. I stood, took the paper from him, and threw it in the trash before walking from the office.

I was frustrated and could not wait to finish the day. I returned to the office that I shared with the ladies and got back to work. I did not call my husband as I had wanted to because I did not want to leave my post! I refused to give off the vibe that I lacked professionalism, or the ability to get back to work after that situation.

Ladies, I had exemplified the unhealthy nature of "Black don't crack." In hindsight, I should have gone to my car and cried while I talked to my husband.

Later, I had to ask myself why I had handled things that way. It should have been okay that I had been affected by that scenario. Yet, as a Black woman, I had felt it necessary to display the "Black don't crack" persona in order to protect "my peace."

Of course, the CNO had come to the office shortly thereafter and asked me a question (I do not remember the question. I just know she came in to talk to me). I turned to her and said, "I don't know. You should ask the CEO." I then went back to my work. I no longer cared what went on, how I reacted, or how she felt about what I had to say. I mean, what could she do to me? Fire me?

I continued with my day. When it was time to leave, I picked up my things and walked out the door. I knew I traveled a path different from others on the "corporate streets." I had to figure out the best way to navigate.

Upon my return to work the next day, I'd been moved from the office I had shared with my colleagues to an office at the front of the hospital, shared with the receptionist. The move signaled what I had known; my time was limited and I had to get out of there. Each day for the next month, I wondered, how much longer was I to remain, and if this was my fault. Had my need to advocate for myself and my patients put me in a position for this type of treatment? Of course, I participated in a personal blame pity party instead of placing full blame on them and seeing their actions as having seen my experience for what it had been—systemic racism.

Sis, that story ended with my falling ill and being rushed to the emergency room as a direct result of the stress that I had experienced. From the moment that had happened, I then realized that I could not return to that job; my Black had cracked.

That experience did not end my journey. I did not have an epiphany and obtain freedom from professional stress when I left the hospital. Part of my journey included going on a self-blame tour, blaming myself for my professional experiences and what I deemed as failures. My career path included changing jobs every six to eight months. Unfortunately, the unspoken rule of staying at a job for at least two years did not help.

Questions from individuals that I knew professionally and personally regarding why I job hopped became the norm. I remember someone asking me, "Why do you run from professional challenges?" Although the questions were tough, I would somehow land jobs with great organizations. Early on in my role, things would go great in and outside of the department I worked in. However, the moment I asked to collaborate, or showed my leadership skills outside of the department, or a coworker expressed any level of disdain toward me, the relationship with leadership abruptly changed. This specifically happened to me when I was on PTO due to my sciatica and could not walk. Once I returned to work, the manager who once supported my professional desires went on an Anti-Alicia campaign that went so far as to tell me that I could not leave work early for my youngest daughter's gymnastics meet! (Y'all know I went to that gymnastics meet, right?)

I wondered if I had become damaged professional goods,

incapable of ever excelling professionally.

You Determine What Encouragement Looks Like For You

From 2016 through 2018, I asked myself what had I done wrong? How had I ended up in this situation? How in the world was I to ensure it didn't happen again? I felt it had to be me and not battling systemic racism.

Let me make this clear, when I worked at the hospital, there had been a white lady no one liked. As far as I knew, she had never been written up, nor received a tough time in the workplace. Employees and management had chosen to talk behind her back rather than share their disdain toward how she managed her work. Considering her treatment, I felt as though management had to keep the "Angry Black Woman" in control and at bay. I'd been given the verbal warning to keep me under control. The stereotype of the angry black woman is not a new phenomenon, instead it's something Black women have had to manage regularly, especially when we decide to speak up and advocate for ourselves4.

I am not perfect, BUT I do know that I am not an Angry Black Woman. I am an educated Black woman—a wife, mother, friend, professional, and more. My intersections, the labels that identify me, are not based on my emotions, reactions, or labels that do not promote positivity or strength.

When talking to friends and sharing war stories, unfortunately our experiences became the rule rather than the exception. However, these conversations validated my feelings that my experiences proved the product of systemic racism. Once I confirmed the root cause, I was able to encourage myself and silence those who failed to validate mine or their professional experience.

I recalled a time I had been told that I "run-away" from tough experiences at work because once I had validated my experiences, I left. I had always viewed my ability to leave situations where I felt abused and mistreated as a strength. Sis, those words did not make me change my strategy. Instead, it made me stop sharing my experiences with that person and any other individual who did not share my point of view when it came to navigating Corporate America. Honestly, I do not know about you, but I'm capable of beating myself up enough without receiving additional help from anyone else.

Once discharged from the hospital, I had to figure out next steps concerning my professional career while protecting my peace and my health. When I speak of health, I mean holistically: mind, body, and spirit. My body cried out for peace that my mind and spirit begged for and I ignored. When I look back on that time my Black was cracking, because I ignored it, my body began to break down.

I had to take a moment to figure out what was going on. To be honest, I blamed myself for what got me here and wondered had I just kept my mouth shut and focused on my job—you know, "shut up and dribble,"—would I be in this situation? I did not validate myself and say, "GIRL, you are not well, and you need to leave this job immediately." I took ownership of how I felt and unfortunately, that was not the right thing to do.

Now let me say this: I was not a victim, and I do not want to portray myself as such. I was a Black woman who had experienced the effects of systemic racism. Systemic racism does not only affect us in our experiences, but it also affects our physical bodies and our mental health23. These people literally had made me sick, and I needed to do whatever I needed to get out of the situation as quickly as possible.

I opted to go on leave-of-absence for the next three months to allow my body to heal and to figure out what to do with myself. I want to make sure that I do not make this timeline seem short. This experience lasted about six months. I never thought I would have to do this. I had thought I was on the right track professionally.

Keeping it Real Type Encouragement

Sis, I'm going to keep it real with you. Leaving an abusive workplace is not easy and is not always the option for many Sistas. Some Sistas stay at their abusive workplace for financial benefit. Sometimes they stay to show that they are not willing to run from a challenging situation, and/or they believe that they need to put in years-of-service to show prospective hiring managers that they have longevity on the job12.

Whatever reason you must stay in a toxic or abusive workplace belongs to you and no one should shame you for that reason. If you are going to stay in a toxic or abusive workplace, I want to encourage you to ask yourself the following questions:

- How can I protect my peace while I am here? Do I have access to a therapist that I can visit regularly and can call during a crisis?

Working in a toxic or abusive environment can change who you are as a person, and you want to make sure that you have a safe space where you can share your experiences confidentially.

- What is my exit strategy?

I recommend that you write out an exit strategy that confirms your exit timeline, what must happen for you to exit prior to your planned date, and what type of outcomes you must obtain prior to your exit. This is a short list. That said, you must confirm what you expect and have a plan in place prior to your exit.

• What type of organization do you want to work for?

Research organizations by going on LinkedIn and reviewing the social structure, how freely employees speak on LinkedIn, and how culturally diverse their organization is. Review the organization's website and social media pages to confirm its culture. Add additional items to your checklist that are important to you.

• What type of role do you want when you leave the toxic environment?

Determine if you want lateral self-promotion or if you want a step-up via self-promotion. Research the skills you need for the promotion you desire and make sure that you obtain those skills while in the toxic or abusive workplace.

Sis, if there are additional aspects needed to prepare you to leave your current organization, please add them to the list. Those aspects should function as an addition to the list above, not-instead of. While on my journey to VEE, I developed this list to determine next steps as I navigated my final toxic and abusive employer. I created a spreadsheet with answers for each bullet point and prepared to put these questions and answers to the test. Because of this list, I exited the toxic environment with validation and encouragement and exited in a way I never imagined. I will say, I obtained some new scars, but I am healed and whole and thankful to have survived and elevated myself professionally.

"

Never turn down the opportunity to network. Your network is truly your net worth. If I had not participated in that initial phone call, I might have missed ou on an opportunity to receive funding fo my organization. That funding propelled me toward 100% entrepreneurship. To this day, I attend events that I gripe about while driving there; however, shortly after attending, I confirm a new line of business or funding for my organization.

-Alicia Coulter

"

Sis, what actions are you putting in place to stay ready for elevation?

Chapter 4

Elevation

As I started writing this chapter, the first thing that came to mind was, "Nothing can stop me. I'm all the way up!"

Sis, it is time to go all the way up. In the previous chapter, I gave you the blueprint on how to remain encouraged as you escape a toxic and/or abusive workplace, and I confirmed what I had to do to level up. Now, it's time to prepare you for elevation. I've elevated my professional life to the point where I am creating Safe Spaces for Black WomenTM and as beautiful as these experiences are, the ability to provide these spaces did not come overnight.

SIS, WHEN YOU ELEVATE, WE ALL ELEVATE

What is Elevation?

Elevation: moving to the next level professionally to spaces that appreciate your Blackness!

Now, I know finding safe spaces that encourage elevation in Corporate America can be challenging; however, you must continue to press forward to find your organization in the same way that you would press forward to find "your person—a friend or partner." When seeking "your person," you want to make sure your values match, because what is important to you should be important to them. The same thought process is inherent when you're looking to elevate professionally[13]. Many of us will not elevate and have not elevated in a traditional way. Whatever path we take, we must make sure that the values that protect our peace and mental health match where we are going professionally.

If You Stay Ready to Elevate, You Do Not Have to Get Ready!

Sis, the good poet Mr. Sugar Free said, "If you stay ready, you don't have to get ready," and I must say, when you want to elevate, this same philosophy must remain in the forefront of your mind. When you think of successful Black women, one of the similarities they all hold is their ability to pivot when their path to success is not moving in the direction that is beneficial for them. For instance, when you think of our current Vice President, Kamala Harris' ascension to the second highest office in the land, recall, she was on the road to the office of the presidency and was doing well. Once her poll numbers shifted, she shifted. Harris dropped out of the race, pivoted to being the candidate for Vice President, and then became the Vice President of the United States of America. Some will say that she did not obtain the role she wanted; however, I contend that she obtained the role she needed to elevate her professional stock.

Sis, what type of pivot do you need to make to elevate your professional stock?

In 2018, I sat in the family room of our home after completing my first quarter in my Executive Master of Public Health program at UCLA. My husband asked me when I planned to focus on going into business for myself? I remember telling him that my goal was to become a Vice President of a Fortune 10 Managed Care Organization so I could obtain a great stock and retirement package. Later that month, I lost my job and decided maybe I should look into initiating the process of forming a Limited Liability Company. I did my due diligence and worked with a graphic artist to design a logo for an organization I thought would operate as a side hustle. I planned it as a side hustle, because remember, my five-year plan had been to become a Vice President within the healthcare industry. I know that my goal was a little lofty, as a Black woman who had yet to have a positive experience in Corporate America, but I thought maybe this time would be different.

Sometimes, we have plans to elevate one way and elevation comes in a different form. When I completed the paperwork for *Advantage Health Now* (the name of my organization that, moving forward, I will refer to it as "she"), She was my "side hustle" that I would work while I continued to move up the corporate ladder. My goal was to receive multiple promotions within the organization that I worked for because I was told that promotion from within is the best way to obtain career success. My mentor would often say, "When you're ready to leave your current organization, other organizations will see that your previous organization valued you enough to promote you."

Sis, we have been trained to allow organizations to determine when and how we elevate. We have to follow their rules perfectly to secure elevation—from the SMART Goals that we must develop, come to agreement with management on, reevaluate during the year, and then evaluate those goals at the end of the fiscal year; or the constant reviewing of the internal website for promotional opportunities; or talking with management within our department to confirm if the creation of a new role for the department presents an opportunity for promotion.

According to the data, over 40% of internal hires for high performing employees fail. The reason for failure includes but is not limited to:

- Employees are not engaged and do not feel stimulated by leadership.

- High performance does not crossover to the new role; employees cannot live up to their potential.

- Development of new hires is given to low level management.

- Assumptions lead people to believe that high potential employees will continue to stick their necks out for the department[23].

Many of these failures are the result of the hiring process being left to the recruiter. The candidate pool is based on the recruiter determining which candidate is worthy of interview. Sis, have you ever received an email or call from a recruiter that asks questions that leave you puzzled? The data from Harvard Business Journal confirmed that I am not alone. Many employers are unable to assess if their hiring practices are effective in hiring top tier candidates. When asked why, they stated, "They do not measure the effectiveness of their hiring practices because measuring employee effectiveness is difficult." Basically, the department that determines who works for the company has autonomy to determine best practices on determining who will work for the organization; let that sink in for a minute14.

About 28% of recruiters and talent acquisition leaders report that internal candidates are top tier and on their radars to fill their current vacancies. They blame this low percentage of the internal employee candidate pool on the lack of internal staff development and the lack of clear career ladders. I find this statistic disheartening. I've always been taught that employers prefer to promote from within. However, when I worked in Corporate America, most of the open requisitions were filled by external talent[14].

The lack of clear career ladders takes me back to PhD Sis in chapter 2, who works in research. Remember her academic experience and mentorship was from top tier researchers; however, her pathway at her current organization remains unclear. Recall that PhD Sis reports to a woman with a non related master's degree, and PhD Sis has multiple related degrees to her position, and may have a buffer placed between her and her current manager based on a recommendation from the consultant. Where does that leave her when it comes time for promotion?

When I asked PhD Sis about her likelihood of promotion, she confirmed that when the director she reports to was promoted, PhD Sis was supposed to receive a promotion at the same time; she did not! When I asked her why, she stated that leadership sabotaged her shortly after having been promoted and placed her in a position that made her present as though she was not management material. As PhD Sis told me this, more questions came to mind, because this scenario is textbook *Discrimination 101*.

My next question was, "Does your director have the same PhD credentials as you, due to this being a research-based program?"

Sis said, "She does not. She has an unrelated master's degree and was not qualified for the position when she was hired."

This shocked me because I have two master's degrees and was always told that to do research at a high level, you must have a PhD. In addition to our Sis' PhD, she shared additional information with me that confirmed that she is being discriminated against, however, this information could identify her and I would never want to do that. What I gathered from my PhD Sis was that her career ladder had not been designed for her, but had been prepared for her white female director who was not as experienced or educated as my PhD Sis.

When Sistas Collectively Took Elevation into Their Own Hands

The experiences of my PhD Sisare why we must take our professional elevation into our own hands. During the COVID-19 Pandemic, many Black women assessed their workplaces for equity and inclusion and determined if working in these spaces was of benefit to them and their mental health. What proved interesting was that the labor market suffered greatly and no one discussed the real reason why. Many blamed it on COVID-19 AND Millennials; however, they forgot to mention that Black women make up much of the workforce at 53%[15].

That said, many, myself included, opted to leave the workforce and start businesses; we returned to school to elevate our academic success. Many of us took a break to weigh our professional options and manage our household obligations with our families, while some of us wanted to protect our peace in the middle of a pandemic. In the final quarter of 2021, the participation of Black women in the workforce decreased over 60%. From September through October 2021, over 180,000 Black women exited the workforce, and in November 2021, an additional 90,000 Black women left. The Board of Labor Statistics provides the following reason for this startling data: "This reversal in labor force reentry is unique to Black women, as women in other racial-ethnic groups continued to regain their footing in the workforce[16]."

The elevation that we saw during the pandemic was forced. Now that we are beyond the pandemic crisis, we need to discuss how we can elevate without crisis mode as the catalyst. The nation paid attention to our labor force exit due to the pandemic. Can we make waves again to encourage Safe Spaces for Black Women™? I believe we can.

During the pandemic, organizations invested money in Diversity, Equity, and Inclusion (DEI) by hiring mostly Black DEI professionals. These professionals developed Business Relation Groups, Affinity Groups, as well as policies and procedures centered in DEI[17].

With these changes, was there any emphasis placed on how Black women were to reenter the workforce safely? In a recent article titled: Creating Safe Spaces for Black Leaders, the director of Provider Services for United Health Group said, "Safe spaces start with leadership, Being able to witness courageous support by an ally then translates to individuals, like myself, feeling reassured that there is authentic support and care being put toward diversity, equity, and inclusion[18]."

Leadership dedicated to DEI is important, especially if an individual can lead from a space of confidence without focusing on microaggressions from others. Creating Safe Spaces for Black Women™ is vital to an organization's success, and when organizations do not realize this fact, sis, it's time for elevation.

How Do I Elevate

In 2020, I participated in the Black Women of Public Health Facebook Group (BWPHFG). I saw a sista post, requesting Black women to share their experiences of exhaustion and how they felt overall during the pandemic. Her post reminded me that In 2014, I published my thesis for my MSW and the challenges I had getting

Black folks to participate in my research. After that experience, I vowed that if I could support another sista in her research, I would. The opportunity presented itself in the BWPHFG, and I did just that.

During the conversation, the researcher and I connected well. Once the questions regarding the research were over, she turned off the camera, and we ran our mouths like we had known each other prior to that conversation. She asked where I worked, and if I were a leader in the organization. Frustrated, I told her that I was not and that I wanted to leave my job but was not sure how to do it. I shared with her that I had an LLC and had been trying to figure out the best way to use it. At the time, I provided health care navigation services to eight clients, but I was not passionate about the work. I had not planned to leave my job to work for myself doing something I was not passionate about.

She told me about funding that was coming down the pipeline and that I should apply for it, so I did. I remember pressing submit and leaving my fate in God's hands. I was nervous and had no clue what I was getting myself into, but I was ready for change. I mean, I have Black Girl Magic. There is nothing I cannot do!Months passed, and I continued working my 9-to-5. My number had grown to ten clients, but I still treated my business like a side hustle.

I want to paint this scene for you: I'm at home, in the kitchen, and my business email dings. It's an email regarding the funding. I take a deep breath and open the email, and then open the attachment. I GOT IT! I fall to my knees and then flat on my face, sobbing and crying. I'll never forget that day. I wish I had a video to share, because it remains a moment to behold.

Our organization was awarded the funding and all I could think was, "Is this enough for me to quit my job?"

To be honest with you Sis, it was not enough; however, this funding elevated me to a space I did not know that I needed to reach. Let me be very clear, sis; my elevation did not occur immediately after the encouragement of receiving funding, but the funding did lead to me devising a plan:

- Never turn down the opportunity to network. Your network is truly your net worth. If I had not participated in that initial phone call, I might have missed out on an opportunity to receive funding for my organization. That funding propelled me toward 100% entrepreneurship. To this day, I attend events that I gripe about while driving there; however, shortly after attending, I confirm a new line of business or funding for my organization.

- Exercise patience. The journey to the top is slow and steady! I know that we want out of our toxic spaces with quickness, however, I can tell you, the more patience I have exercised, the better my opportunities.

- Follow the blueprint provided in the encouragement chapter. Using those steps kept me grounded and focused on my goals. I believe they will do the same for you. Elevation is truly about the work that you put in when you are experiencing your lowest professional point.

Let me say that again.

ELEVATION IS ABOUT THE WORK THAT YOU PUT IN WHEN YOU ARE AT YOUR LOWEST PROFESSIONAL POINT.

If you can do the work to encourage yourself when you are at your lowest professional point, then you will have the strength you need to elevate.

Now, sis, I am an entrepreneur and I know that is not the pathway for every sis reading this book. Therefore, what elevation looks like for you, is determined by you. Remember, I thought elevation would happen for me when I obtained a Vice President role for a Fortune 10 company. Now, elevation looks like making my own schedule, having the title of CEO, being a decision maker for multiple organizations that are owned by my family and I, and not having to navigate any obstacles within Corporate America.

What does elevation look like for you? Review the bullet points in the "encouragement chapter" and use those answers to determine your version of elevation.

As you determine what elevation looks like for you, remember:

Elevation is About the Work That You Put in When You Are at Your Lowest Professional Point.

> Sis, do we really know
> our professional strength
> as Black women within
> the workplace?

-Alicia Coulter

Sis, do YOU know your own strength?

Chapter 5

Creating a New Environment

Sis, in the encouragement chapter, I talked about the parallel between finding your person and finding a job.

I want to dig deeper into this subject because I understand the importance of courting your employer or client to reduce the risk of you placing yourself in spaces that are not safe for Black women. Also, you do not want to undo the work that you did when you validated, encouraged, and elevated yourself. Unfortunately, we must take ownership of the spaces we place ourselves in because we are the decision makers of our lives. I wish we did not have to take on any of the responsibility, that society would make room for us and protect us. Truthfully, society should take ownership of developing and perpetuating spaces that are safe for Black women, but until then, we must take care of ourselves.

Have you ever taken an offer for a job without doing your due diligence regarding the culture, brand, diversity, pathway to elevation, validation, encouragement, and additional things that are important to you? I have, and I regret it completely.

For my last role in Corporate America (at the healthcare company) the only criteria I had was being close to home; that's it! Using that guideline as my determining factor was not enough. I wish I'd had the encouragement list at that time, because that job had so many red flags. The red flags were not obvious immediately. Well, maybe they were, but I ignored them because the recruiter was a Black man, and we'd had great convos when I spoke to him. After our first meeting, he scheduled an interview for a Sr. Program Manager role. I remember my excitement, because not only was the job close to home, but it was also around the corner from my husband's job. After the panel interview, months passed. My emails went ignored, and then finally, I heard from the recruiter. He told me that the group had really liked me, but that they did not have a role for me and the position had closed. Later, he called, offering another interview opportunity. I took the call, interviewed for the job, and received an offer within three weeks. Of course, I took the job, because, remember, I was so basic with my requirements. I am kinda embarrassed; however, I am hoping I can encourage others not to make this mistake, especially those of us with kiddies.

Sis, this next line is what trapped me into the position without having any additional criteria. The recruiter said, "Alicia, we need more Black people here, so I'm going to get you hired. When I get you hired, do not worry about the position. I'm going to get your promotion within eight months of your hire date."

Siiis, didn't that line sound like someone who wants to be my partner, but is not ready for commitment, but wants to show me a good time, and that I wouldn't know he was *running game* until it was too late?

When I was in this "situation," I did not view my experience from that lens, but I do now. I am sharing this with you so that you too have that lens. Entering a professional relationship based on a promise that is not written in a contract is not a supportable, professional relationship. Six to eight months went by. I sent the Black man a message on *Teams*. He ignored the message. I then emailed him, and he ignored that as well. I became a bit anxious because he had not responded to me. Finally, when he did respond, he acted brand new like we hadn't had a verbal agreement. Weeks after that interaction, he reached out to my personal email and told me that he had been FIRED.

Sis, the Black man who had lost his job, told me to send him my resume for another job at a different organization. I replied with condolences and moved on.

I was so angry and distraught over my experience that I had to pour myself a glass of wine. His email basically told me that I was stuck at this trash job, with no sign of promotion. I allowed that man to control my elevation. When I look back on the situation, instead of allowing it to anger me, I now use it as a lesson: "Never let anyone control your elevation, Alicia!" I am also telling you, never let anyone control your elevation, Sis!

Before making this next statement, let me stress that I am not offering legal advice. I am sharing information for educational purposes only. As previously mentioned, entering a professional relationship based on a promise, one that is not written in a contract, is not a strong relationship—especially if you do not know your rights. Had I known that if I'd informed HR of the verbal agreement the recruiter made with me, I may have possibly been promoted within the timeframe the Black man quoted me[19].

The only reason I do not believe this would have helped me 100% is: I questioned if HR would have believed me. Even if they hadn't, I wish I knew, so that I could have shared it with HR on the record.

Sis, I share this story with you because I allowed that Black man to determine my professional environment, versus me creating my own professional environment. The relationship that I had with the organization started on a bad note during the interview process, and although I needed a job, I needed to ask this question: "Did I

85

need THAT job?" Now, I'd ask myself, "Was that job my person?" I can truly say no, that job was not "my person." As I navigated through the professional experiences I had with various jobs, I wondered, "Did I do what I needed to do to create a safe space for myself?" Of note, I did not have the encouragement checklist at the point of being hired for this job; however, I have it now. As a result, I am creating environments that are for us, and by us. That is what makes all of what I have experienced worth it.

Do We Know Our Power

All week I'd been singing Whitney Houston's song, "Didn't Know My Own Strength." Sis, do we really know our professional strength as Black women within the workplace? Remember, we make up over 50% of the workforce yet we are treated the worst[20].

Do we have the power to shift this by creating environments that are best for our mental health and safety? Are these environments solely professional or do we have to create personal spaces that are safe for Black women, or can we do both? Throughout the writings in this book, my mind often shifts back to the experiences of our PhD Sis and what she continues to experience at work. She is truly a dope Sista, and I wonder if she knows her strength. I believe that she does. She knows the power that she possesses. I believe like me, and many of us, she is allowing passion for what she does to determine her environment.

During our conversation, she made a statement that shook me to my core; "they [professional institutions] will burn down a whole city to protect a white woman even if it causes the entire project to fail."

When she said that, my brain churned and I thought, "Will we as Black women stay in the environment to put out the fire? Do we take a level of ownership in an environment that was created 'for them by us' (FTBU) to the point where we suffer and lose the ability to *know our own strength (and power)?*"

One way that we can use our power in the workplace is through individuals who we have labeled allies. This alignment can benefit us because white people continue to hold the most power in the workplace[20]. Use those who desire allyship to benefit you and other Black women within the workplace. I want to make it very clear, I don't mean blindly trust white people in the workplace. In my experience, some have been abusive to Black women in every environment that we navigate. My goal in sharing this with you is to encourage a level of strategy, so that you can create safety within your workplace. The same strategies can be used for women who are entrepreneurs. I have relationships with white women who provide me with professional elevation through providing business and funding opportunities. Knowing that these *professional* relationships with white people can exist, we should use the relationships to our benefit by using the tools below:

- Use Strategy. Strategically, find the social group that is most willing to work with Black women in the workplace and assess their willingness to provide allyship to Black women. These are the "I voted for Obama" people, or the people who awkwardly smile at you in hopes that you'll speak to them.

- Be Patient. Do not share too quickly your plan or your need for allyship. Allow that to come naturally, based on their seeing your experiences in the workplace.

- Focus on allyship with senior leadership ONLY. You need to collaborate with individuals who have a pen and a purse. Those individuals hold leadership roles that can sign contracts and write checks!

I know a woman who uses this strategy, and she rarely experiences unsafe workspaces. When and if she does, she has an ally to help her navigate the less desirable situations. I remember thinking once that she was a sellout for using these strategies, because I was one who opted not to align professionally with white people (I'm sure my experiences confirm why). After watching her from afar, I saw that she not only benefited from allyship in her current space, but also was able to develop relationships that made it easy for her to leave a job, transition into a new position, with a more grandiose title, more perks, and mo' money, mo' money, mo' money! This Sis knew her power and used it to her benefit.

Now, if you're like me, you're going to have a level of discomfort aligning with white people at work because they make it difficult, PERIOD. I say that unapologetically because of the trauma they have inflicted on Black people in their workplaces. If this power dynamic challenges you, I encourage you to develop safe spaces in your personal life. These safe spaces can act as a buffer and help increase your network and your NET WORTH.

Creating Safe Spaces for Black Women™

I want to be honest with you, because Sis, I am not one to sugar coat the truth. For Black women to obtain safe spaces, creating them professionally or personally can come with challenges. In professional spaces, leadership may have a level of fear commensurate with the backlash associated with spotlighting the need to protect Black women. This is where allyship and patience comes into play. When presenting the need for these spaces, you can use the same framework that was used to prove the need for Employee/Business Relationship Groups. Your leadership should also possess an awareness of the data associated with Black women being discriminated against in the workplace more than any other ethnic group. One of the key findings from Catalyst, a group of anti-racism leaders is, "Women with darker skin tones are more likely than women with lighter skin tones to experience racism at work[21]."

Sis, there is a plethora of data available to prove the need for these safe spaces due to the racism and anti-Blackness within the workplace.

When creating these spaces, they must be presented with a structure of Black women at the helm. Black women must organize and lead these spaces. This is not the time for allies to show their understanding of Black women's experiences within the workplace. We need them to stand guard when the haters try to shut down the safe space!

I created Safe Spaces for Black Women™ professionally, and I remember the first time I did so. The leader within the organization that I communicated with was a Black woman. She worked under the leadership of a white woman who agreed with the need to develop an intentional safe space for the Black women within the organization. Generally, my safe spaces recur weekly for five weeks; however, this client was able to budget for a full day's experience of validation, encouragement, and elevation of Sistas within their workplace. We also gave them a gift to provide them with self-care, and to remind them of the value they bring to the workplace. These women cried from the experience and wanted to know when we planned to return for part two. Their responses fueled me to continue to enhance the programming. I have since developed and executed a program that lasts five weeks, which has provided a longer lasting experience for the women who have participated.

I want to make sure that I am forthright and honest with you. I've presented my program and have confirmed several clients;

however, when I am rejected because leadership is fearful of what non-Black employees will say, I am often frustrated and disappointed that protecting Black women is politicized within the workplace. I am not surprised by these actions; however, their actions do not reduce the need for these organizations to protect and promote Black women as well as provide safe spaces for us[22]!

I understand that every Black woman is not in a workplace that is willing to provide this support or is an entrepreneur that works in a silo. I encourage you to develop a safe space within your personal environments. These spaces can look like a group of Sister friends, or present as events that are for Black women and by Black women. I've created these Safe Spaces for Black Women™ in the Los Angeles Area and on virtual platforms, and the benefits of these spaces can be seen on the faces of the women.

One attendee said, "Black women need a space to get together, let our hair down, take our shoes off, and talk about us… UNFILTERED!! We NEED this!! I appreciate Alicia creating this space for us. We deserve luxury and that's exactly what we've been able to experience."

Sis, I never thought that the professional and personal spaces would receive so much positive feedback. The idea of creating **Safe Spaces for Black Women™** was created in my living room while my hairstylist was braiding my hair. I was nervous and afraid, but I knew that these spaces were necessary for us—by us! When creating these new environments, I knew the benefits would outweigh the risks. Even in knowing that, I had to confirm the benefits.

Validation: Black women securing a welcoming space, where all of their perceptions of their experiences are welcomed—no harm by, or to any woman in the space would occur.

Encouragement: These spaces provide Black women with support, joy, and confidence giving Black women a positive experience.

Elevation: Elevating Black women should include networking opportunities with professional Black women, as well as the ability to foster friendships, create new memories, and a sense of fellowship.

All of these spaces are Black women only. Once a Sista enters **Safe Spaces for Black Women™**, she is taking ownership of her experience and her takeaway.

> **"**
> Finding your safe space in
> corporate America takes the same
> energy as finding your person.
>
> -Alicia Coulter

Sis, how will you use strategy, patience, and
allyship to create a new and
safe environment?

Conclusion

This book is more than a space for me to share my truth and the truths of other Black women. This book serves as a toolkit to validate, encourage, and elevate the professional lives of Black women. Forever, we have been told that we are angry, we like to use the "race card." We have been made to feel as though our Black is a barrier to our successes. Society encourages us to continue to navigate these spaces without protection from harm and/or a safe space for us to land. We are also encouraged to ignore the behaviors of bigots and racist, or to internalize our feelings towards their behaviors. Unfortunately, this is status quo and many of us continue to experience harm without a safe space.

The harm we face challenges our ability to navigate Corporate America safely and causes stressors that harm our physical and mental health. Terms like "Black Don't Crack" are often used to describe our shell and the beauty that we exhibit as Black women. Although our external Blackness does defy the odds, our internal Blackness is steadily cracking under the weight of systemic racism and causing us professional and personal harm.

While writing this book, I had moments of tears and breakdowns because of the pain and emotion that Sistas shared with me regarding their experiences. Their stories gave me flashbacks of my professional experiences. One Sista told me that after continued workplace abuse, she finally came to the realization that she had to stop putting loyalty into a place it did not belong.

In the introduction, I shared my encounters with behaviors that caused my Black to crack, and my having to use life's oil to rejuvenate my Black. One of life's oils that I used was developing **Safe Spaces for Black Women™**. Prior to creating safe spaces, I had to work on myself to confirm MY WHY, why I needed a safe space as a Black woman. I know that sounds crazy, right? That said, because often we are placed in unsafe spaces, we start to normalize the accompanying experiences and forget that harm is not the norm.

Sis, you must determine your why. What was *my* why? My why was because I deserved it! I deserved a space that allowed me to walk with confidence and beauty. I deserved a space that allowed me to stand free from stress, and free from harm. Once I confirmed my why, I was able to create and successfully execute VEE for myself!

Validation

The job that forced me to start working on VEE was the job at the hospital with the Ronald Regan loving Republican. Having experienced illness due to the stress and anxiety from that job, I knew that I needed to regroup and figure out how to never allow another job to literally make me sick! I began to validate myself and tell myself that I am *wonderfully made; designed with loving care.* I had to confidently say those things to myself because that was and still is the truth. The experiences that I encountered were the result of my Blackness.

Validation is the first and most important step of VEE. In order to move confidently into your safe space, you must confirm that your current space is unsafe because of how you perceive it. In confirming the lack of safety, you are able to set boundaries for yourself and those boundaries will keep you from reentering into unsafe spaces. My Sis in the validation chapter, who went on leave-of-absence, transitioned to a new job that paid less money. Recall, she said that she was not going back to the corporate workforce and would work for herself as a licensed therapist. She also confirmed that there is no need for her to continue in unsafe environments—environments that do not care about us. When she told me that, I almost cried because her words proved that when you acknowledge and validate your experiences, you begin the journey to creating safe spaces for yourself. As Black women, the safe space starts with and within us.

Validation is not the only work that must be done to create a safe space for yourself. After I validated my experience at the hospital, I did not immediately enter a safe space. VEE was executed at a snail's pace for me, Sis. WhenI look back at my professional experiences, I sometimes want to beat myself up for taking so long to validate my experiences, encourage myself, and elevate professionally. But as I write this book, I know that my journey through VEE to the space I am now was for you, and that makes it worth it.

I have shared my experience of getting to VEE and what a safe space looks like from a Sista who suffered from workplace violence and abuse. My goal is to continue to confirm that there is life after workplace abuse.

After I left the hospital, I started job hopping. I never fit in anywhere that I went, and I often wondered why. THEN, I assessed the environments in which I worked. Often, I was one of two Black women in my department or the entire organization. Without another Black woman within the space, shared experiences were nonexistent. Staff looked to me to validate all things BLACK; y'all know that role within the department is exhausting.

As I continued to assess why spaces were unsafe for me, I realized that many times those who challenge us, often see our greatness present, yet unexpressed, and it threatens them. When I look at my professional life in the present time, I've realized that these people had to have seen the greatness that lived within me, greatness that I didn't know existed. Sometimes we've called people like them "haters." I often brushed off that word, until I realized there are really people who want to see you lose and hate to see you win! When this occurs against Black women in Corporate America, it stifles our growth and ability to navigate spaces professionally.

Encouragement

Sis, encouragement has been the hardest part for me, because I am hard on myself. I blamed myself for many of the professional situations that I have been in and opted not to show myself any grace. I functioned as though my Black never cracked and as though I could survive any situation. I labeled myself as the "Nice Black Girl" to make sure I seemed as though I appeared "easy to manage." I learned the hard way not to present myself as something I could not uphold. To present myself other than as myself had me in the hospital in pain, sick mentally and physically, and looking like crap. During that time in my life, I couldn't see beyond the moment. I remember wondering what was I to do with this education and professional experience that I acquired but was not appreciated. Where, professionally, would I find safety in the workplace while having an opportunity to show my value as a dedicated employee. I remember my husband asking me why I sought what I needed from Corporate America. I always paused when he asked me that question because I did not see myself as he saw me. From day one, he saw me doing great things professionally, and I thought the great thing was that Vice President gig for a top tier organization. He saw beyond that for me, and it was time that I started to let him and anyone else that I trusted encourage me.

Well, encouragement came when I filled out the paperwork for my LLC, Advantage Health Now. This was after the hospital job, after the job immediately following the hospital. Heck! This came about two years later. There was a point during this timeframe where job hopping was my career path, versus working. I was okay with that. Job hopping allowed me not to get too close to people and reduced the risk of being unsafe. Unfortunately, that did not work; however, it further cemented my need to get out of the unsafe spaces where I continued to place myself.

Remember, I said validation, encouragement, or elevation might come from external forces? Mine came from my hubby and one of my favorite Sorors, Crystal D. Williams. Both stayed on me to get out of Corporate America, but I WOULD NOT listen! I literally said, "Where is my paycheck coming from?" or, "You know the lifestyle I like to live. Who is going to make sure I can live my lifestyle?"

Neither my hubby or Crystalwere interested in what I was saying. They both pushed me and supported me to make big money moves outside of Corporate America. I remember Crystal saying, "Alicia, why don't you just leave your job?" and I laughed so hard. Although she was sincere, I thought that request was beyond funny.

It wasn't until 2018 I finally listened to their encouragement and started the LLC paperwork. In an earlier chapter, I discussed the clients and the funding. During this time, I was working, so I had my salary plus the funding and client money. However, I was still dealing with workplace abuse and my hubby and Crystal telling me to escape Alcatraz. Okay, I'm being silly; Corporate America (real talk, I often felt like I was locked up). BUT THE MONEY WAS GOOD!! I brought in six figures from my job, money from my clients, and my salary from the funding we received. Why in the world would I leave that?

Sis, when I look back on that time, and what happened, I wonder what value I placed on myself? Was my peace no longer priceless? The encouragement from my hubby and Crystal started to work, and I went on leave-of-absence. I was not ready to leave my six-figure job, but I was ready to take a break from it to see if either was right.

Shhh, do not tell my hubby or Crystal I applied for other jobs and interviewed. Do you know that none of those jobs hired me? I felt sabotaged! I think My Husband prayed that I wouldn't get a new job.

While I was on leave-of-absence, I did not work hard to create a structure for my LLC. I can tell you, my hubby continued to lovingly encourage me. Sis, I enjoyed being off work and not having to deal with meetings, silly questions about my hair or the infamous, "how can you afford the car that you drive?" Yes, Sis, someone in my department asked me that question.

I enjoyed the break, but break time was over. It was time for me to put the encouragement from my hubby and Crystal into the forefront of my mind and get to work. I posted on social media, developed my website with my Brand Manager, and everything else you must do to develop an organization. I'm not sure if my hubby and Crystal know the depth of their encouragement, however, I want them to know their encouragement fueled me.

Once my business started booming, I forgot all about that job and

I was at a crossroad: do I return to work, or do I leave? I worked remotely, so I thought, "Eh, I can return to work and just work remotely and not see their faces." Then I was reminded that the workplace abuse I experienced happened while working remotely!

I decided it was time for me to leave, and so I left. I got up out of there! Once I did, my business started to thrive, to the point where I needed to add lines of business, hire contract staff, consultants, and subcontractors to manage the business that I could not manage. The level of encouragement that I received helped me to get on to a path that I did not think I needed or deserved. It's clear to me now that I needed and deserved the encouragement.

Sis, do you have someone in your space to encourage you when you have had enough? If not, I want to encourage you. Your path is laid for you already. You just have to get on it and go! What is the worst thing that can happen, a detour!? Girl, get on the path of success and find out. You can do this. It's all about you! You know that where you are right now is not for you, and you need to stop forcing it! Take the break, so that you can develop the greatness that is in you!

Honestly, my encouragement for Black women knows no limit! In my mind, and from what I can see, there is nothing that we cannot do.

Sometimes, encouragement looks just like self-affirmation "on my mama, on my hood, I LOOK FLY. I LOOK GOOD... touch my swag, with you would!" Get into it, give yourself exactly what you need to encourage yourself.

Elevation

Finally, the elevation!!! I feel like a pastor. "I'm going to shout, because I know what I am going to say." Honestly, elevation is my favorite part of VEE, because I know what it takes to get here. Sleepless nights, frustration, hurt, pain, mistakes, false hope, you name it, these activities and feelings occur. I want to call them growing pains, but I do not know if that is what they are. I want to call the entire process "pain and suffering," because that is what I experienced. When you experience something that is as dense as what you experience during workplace abuse, you are literally experiencing pain and you are suffering mentally, physically, and emotionally.

That said, we can use strength-based methodology and call them growing pains as we focus on ascending into elevation from the space of validation and encouragement. I just know when I went through it, I did not want to call my experience growing pains. I was literally in pain, crying, and just downright miserable.

Before I move forward explaining my path to elevation, let me tell you, elevation did not come overnight for me. I was determined to get out of these unsafe spaces. Sometimes, I focused on ME and not my healing. I was focused on making sure the money was right. Had I known that elevation brings career success, I would have focused on completing VEE in a faster way.

When I left my job to move on, I was nervous. The validation and encouragement that I received was good, but I now needed to focus on being a business owner without a job to fall back on. I was attentive to my current businesses. I made sure to cultivate my reputation in the professional communities that I networked in, because remember, your network is your net worth. As I networked, I realized there were Black women who did not need a coaching program. They did not need group therapy; they needed a safe space for a Black woman. A space where Sis can come and just be Sis with other Sistas.

When I created this space, I cried. I FINALLY MADE IT. My calling was here, and I answered the phone! I did not run away from my successes; I met them head on, and I'm thankful that I did. I do not want to make it seem as though I was not nervous, because I was. But what could I lose? I had already had horrible workplace experiences.

Elevation is not about when to elevate, but how to elevate. Remember the steps to encouragement steer you toward elevation, and you want your elevation to be long lasting.

One of the biggest issues the individuals within my professional space had with me was associated with my ability to assert my knowledge within my career, without any fear of what any of these people might do to me. They saw my ability to elevate before I did.

Sis, I started this book the same way that I am ending it, with a story of workplace abuse that changed my perspective of Corporate America. The difference is, I have validated, encouraged, and elevated myself and with that, I am creating **Safe Spaces for Black Women™**. Unfortunately, so many Sistas have yet to experience a safe space professionally and continue to have to navigate difficult spaces. I want to first validate you, Sis. Your experience is exactly what you say it is. No one can take that from you. I know that validating your experiences can be difficult. It took me years to do so. Know that once you validate yourself, you are on the road to your safe space. I want to encourage you. You are wonderfully made and I want you to know that in your being validated and encouraged; you are on your way to elevation.

> **"**
> My family thrives when
> I am safe; I must remain free from
> harm for mine and their well-being
> -Alicia Coulter

Sis, why do you DESERVE a safe space?

SAFE SPACES
For Black Women

ABOUT THE AUTHOR

Alicia Coulter, MPH, MSW is the is a highly sought after advocate and public speaker focusing her work in protecting the lives of Black women. She is also the CEO & Co-Founder AHN Foundation, a nonprofit that is committed to providing Safe Spaces for Black Women™ and health equity and inclusive services to the Black community. Her desire to develop Safe Spaces for Black Women™ was birthed from her habitually experiencing unsafe spaces in corporate America because of her being a Black woman. The spaces that she creates afford Black women a space that is for Black women by a Black woman, luxurious, filled with positivity, joy, and sisterhood.

Alicia is also the CEO & Co-Founder of Harmony Development Associates (HDevA), an organization that supports the organizational development efforts of for profit and nonprofit organizations. Her personal experiences with workplace abuse and desire to create her own lane encouraged her to write Safe Spaces for Black Women. Alicia is a native of South Central Los Angeles and resides in the Suburbs of Los Angeles County with her husband of 22 years and three "almost grown." daughters.

> " Black women are deserving of luxury and deserve to feel safe!
> -Alicia Coulter

> Creating Safe Spaces for Black Women™ is not just about good food and music, it is about sisterhood and the experience of being in fellowship in a safe space with Black women.

-Alicia Coulter

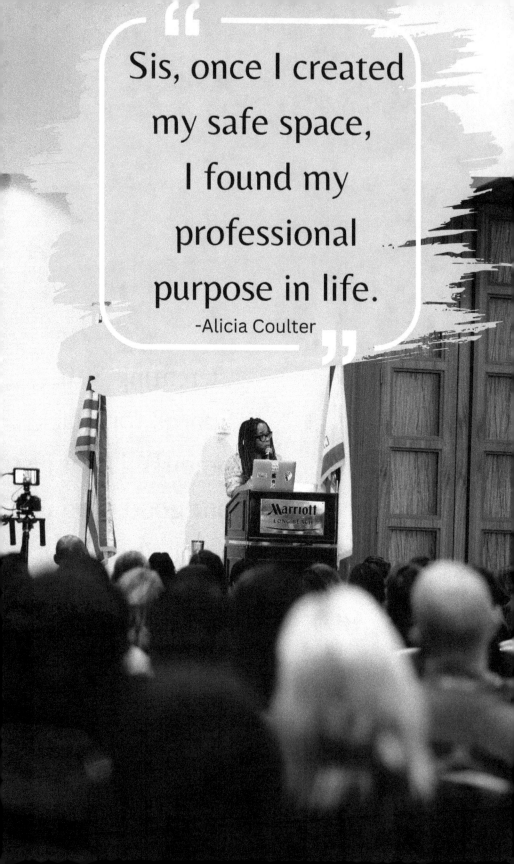

> " Sis, once I created my safe space, I found my professional purpose in life.
> -Alicia Coulter "

As we elevate, the support and encouragement of sister friends provides us the safety we desire.

-Alicia Coulter

> **"**
> Safe Spaces for
> Black Women™ is
> more than words, it
> is a movement!
> -Alicia Coulter

> **"**
> On my mama, on my hood... I mean, if I do not love myself, who will? Love yourself, Sis!
> -Alicia Coulter

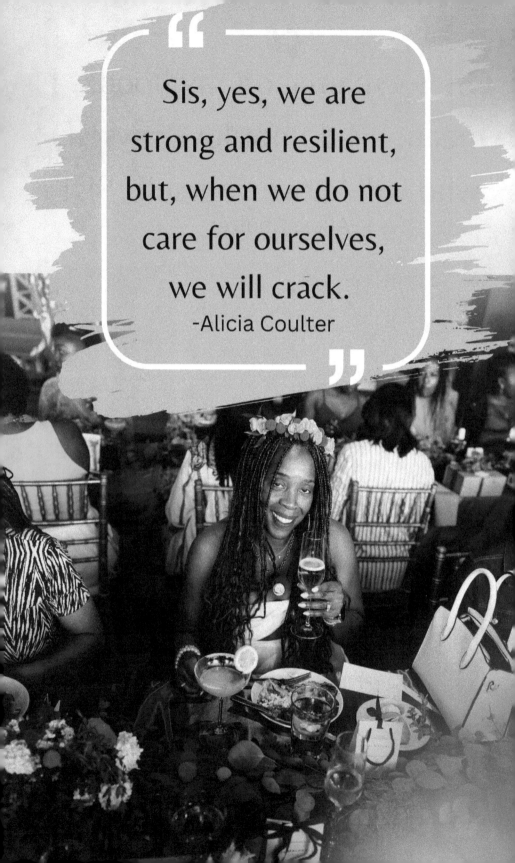

References

1. Abrams, A. (2020, July 17). Amid Social Upheaval and COVID-19, Black Women Create Their Own Health Care Support Networks. Time. https://time.com/5866854/black-women-health-care/
2. National Centers for Education Statistics. (N.D.). Degrees conferred by race/ethnicity and sex. IES>NCES. https://nces.ed.gov/FastFacts/display.asp?id=72
3. Rice, J. (2021, June 22). The Gap Between Minority Experience & White Perceptions of Racism at Work. Forbes. https://www.forbes.com/sites/forbeseq/2021/06/22/the-gap-between-minority-experience--white-perceptions-of-racism-at-work/?sh=4bb616e4240b
4. Matro, D., Evans, J. B., Ellis, Aleksander, P.J., Benson III, L. (2022, January 31). The "Angry Black Woman" Stereotype at Work. Harvard Business Review. https://hbr.org/2022/01/the-angry-black-woman-stereotype-at-work
5. Roux, M. (2021, August 3). 5 Facts About Black Women in the Labor Force. U.S. Department of Labor Blog. https://blog.dol.gov/2021/08/03/5-facts-about-black-women-in-the-labor-force
6. Detert, J., Morang Roberts, L. (2020, July 16). How to Call Out Racial Injustice at Work. Harvard Business Review. https://hbr.org/2020/07/how-to-call-out-racial-injustice-at-work

7. Essence. (2023, July 26). Nearly 40% of Black Women Have Quit Jobs Because They Didn't Feel Emotionally Safe. Essence. https://www.essence.com/news/money-career/black-women-unsafe-workplace-quit-identity/

8. Hunter – Gadsden, L. (2018, November 6). The Troubling News About Black Women in the Workplace. Next Avenue. https://www.nextavenue.org/black-women-workplace/

9. Minority Health. (2023, September 18). Racism is a Serious Threat to the Public's Health. Center for Disease Control. https://www.cdc.gov/minorityhealth/racism-disparities/index.html

10. Hunt, J. (Summer 2021). Maternal Mortality Among Black Women in the United States. Ballard Brief. https://ballardbrief.byu.edu/issue-briefs/maternal-mortality-among-black-women-in-the-united-states#:~:text=A%202014–2016%20national%20study%20on%20pregnancy-related%20deaths%20in,Black%20women%20243%25%20higher%20than%20for%20White%20women

11. Connley, C. (2022, August 24). Over 80% of White Employees See Themselves as Allies at Work, but Black women and Latinas Disagree. CNBC. https://www.cnbc.com/2020/08/21/over-80percent-of-white-employees-see-themselves-as-allies-but-black-women-and-latinas-disagree.html

12. Ways, S. (2018, June 11). 8 Reasons Why Employees Stay In Toxic Organizations. LinkedIn. https://www.linkedin.com/pulse/8-reasons-why-employees-stay-toxic-organizations-susan-ways-sphr/

13. Vyas, S. (2020, February 22). 6 Reasons Why Job Hunting Is Exactly Like Dating (And It Stinks). Work It Daily. https://www.workitdaily.com/job-hunting-is-like-dating/2-there-are-commitment-issues

14. Cappelli, P. (2019). Your Approach to Hiring is All Wrong. Harvard Business Review. https://hbr.org/2019/05/your-approach-to-hiring-is-all-wrong

15. TED: The Economics Daily. (2019, February 26). Black Women Made Up 53 Percent of the Black Labor Force in 2018. U.S. Bureau of Labor Statistics. https://www.bls.gov/opub/ted/2019/black-women-made-up-53-percent-of-the-black-labor-force-in-2018.htm#:~:text=Since%20the%201970s%2C%20women%20have%20made%20up%20an,percent%20of%20the%20total%20labor%20force%20in%202018

16. Barr, A., Henry-Nickle, M., Broady, K. (2021, December 8). The November Jobs Report Shows Black Women are Leaving the Labor Force. Brookings. https://www.brookings.edu/articles/the-november-jobs-report-shows-black-women-are-leaving-the-labor-force/

17. Maurer, R. (2022, August 6). New DE&I Roles Spike After Racial Justice Protest. SHRM. https://www.shrm.org/resourcesandtools/hr-topics/talent-acquisition/pages/new-dei-roles-spike-after-racial-justice-protests.aspx

18. Lindauer, S. (N.D.). How to Create Safe Spaces for Black Leaders. UnitedHealth Group. https://powertofly.com/up/account-manager-at-rtb-house

19. Mukherji, A. (2019, March 21). Promised a Raise? Is It Legally Enforcement. FindLaw. https://www.findlaw.com/legalblogs/law-and-life/promised-a-raise-is-it-legally-enforceable/

20. Lean In. (2020). The State of Black Women in Corporate America. Lean In. https://leanin.org/research/state-of-black-women-in-corporate-america/introduction

21. Eskrine, S., Brassel, S., Robotham, K. (N.D.) Exposé of Women's Workplace Experiences Challenges Antiracist Leaders to Step Up. https://www.catalyst.org/reports/antiracism-workplace-leadership/

22. Jackson, A. (2022, July 1). Black Women are in 'Survival Mode' at Work – and Company Diversity Efforts 'Fall Short." https://www.cnbc.com/2022/07/01/company-diversity-efforts-to-support-black-women-fall-short.html

Printed in the USA
CPSIA information can be obtained
at www.ICGtesting.com
CBHW041522141223
2645CB00008B/409